Science

BIOLOGY

FOR COMMON ENTRANCE

Ron Pickering

GALORE PARK

AN HACHETTE UK COMPANY

The publishers would like to thank the following for permission to reproduce copyright material:
Photo credits

b = bottom, m = middle, t = top, r = right, l = left

Cover photo © panuruangjan/Fotolia **pvii** © Jacek Chabraszewski/Fotolia **px** © MNStudio/Fotolia **p12l** © Dr Gopal Murti/Science Photo Library **p12r** © Claude Nuridsany & Marie Perennou/Science Photo Library **p13** © Dr Gopal Murti/Science Photo Library **p19** © RTimages/Fotolia **p22** © Crown copyright **p31l** © Ammentorp/Fotolia **p31m** © Ammentorp/Fotolia **p31r** © Ammentorp/Fotolia **p32** © Anatolii/Fotolia **p40** © UWimages/Fotolia **p46l** © D. Phillips/Science Photo Library **p46r** © CNRI/Science Photo Library **p48b** © Famveldman/Fotolia **p48t** © shironosov/istock/Thinkstock **p56** © ThorstenSchmitt/Thinkstock **p70** © Przemek Klos/Fotolia **p76t** © Jeffrey Blackler/Alamy **p76b** © draghicich/Thinkstock **p85** © Kmiragaya/Fotolia **p105** © Rugco/Fotolia **p108** © Mikael Rinnan/Thinsktock **p109b** © Protopic/Fotolia **p113** © Friedberg/Fotolia **p117** © O.DIGOIT/Alamy **p120** © Konstandinos/Fotolia **p128l** © Lionel Bret/Look at Sciences/Science Photo Library **p128r** © Photos.com/Thinkstock **p129t** © Natural History Museum, London/Science Photo Library **p129b** © Natural History Museum, London/Science Photo Library **p130t** © Erik Lam/Fotolia **p130b** © EcoView/Fotolia **p131** © Hydrangea100/Thinkstock **p138l** © Lawrence Lawry/Science Photo Library **p138r** © Barbara Strnadova/Science Photo Library

p100, p103b, p103t, p106, p107t, p107b, p109t, p111, p115b, p115t, p125t, p125mt, p125mb, p125b, p128m and p139 © Ron Pickering

Acknowledgements

Extracts on p112 and p113 © Crown copyright. The Nature Conservancy Council publication, *Points of View*. Permission for re-use of all © Crown copyright information is granted under the terms of the Open Government Licence (OGL).

Every effort has been made to trace all copyright holders, but if any have been inadvertently overlooked the publishers will be pleased to make the necessary arrangements at the first opportunity.

Although every effort has been made to ensure that website addresses are correct at time of going to press, Galore Park cannot be held responsible for the content of any website mentioned in this book. It is sometimes possible to find a relocated web page by typing in the address of the home page for a website in the URL window of your browser.

Hachette UK's policy is to use papers that are natural, renewable and recyclable products and made from wood grown in sustainable forests. The logging and manufacturing processes are expected to conform to the environmental regulations of the country of origin.

Orders: please contact Bookpoint Ltd, 130 Milton Park, Abingdon, Oxon OX14 4SB. Telephone: +44 (0)1235 827827. Lines are open 9.00a.m.–5.00p.m., Monday to Saturday, with a 24-hour message answering service. Visit our website at www.galorepark.co.uk for details of other revision guides for Common Entrance, examination papers and Galore Park publications.

Published by Galore Park Publishing Ltd

An Hachette UK company

Carmelite House, 50 Victoria Embankment, London, EC4Y 0DZ

www.galorepark.co.uk

Text copyright © Ron Pickering 2015

The right of Ron Pickering to be identified as the author of this Work has been asserted by him in accordance with sections 77 and 78 of the Copyright, Designs and Patents Act 1988.

Impression number 10 9 8 7

2019

Typeset in 11.5/13 ITC Officina Sans/Book by Integra Software Services Pvt. Ltd, Pondicherry, India.

Printed in India

New illustrations by Integra Software Services Pvt. Ltd, Pondicherry, India.

Some illustrations by Graham Edwards were re-used. The publishers will be pleased to make the necessary arrangements with regard to these illustrations at the first opportunity.

A catalogue record for this title is available from the British Library.

ISBN: 9781471846984

About the author

Ron Pickering has published a number of very successful books covering the GCSE, IGCSE and A level syllabi and has worked in both maintained and independent education for more than 30 years. He now divides his time between teacher training, both in the UK and overseas, and writing, and has been a science advisor and curriculum manager at Altrincham Grammar School for Girls, as well as a Science Inspector for OFSTED.

Ron extends his interest in science by spending many hours photographing animals, both in the wild and in captive environments, and tries to maintain some level of fitness by off-road cycling.

Dedication

I dedicate this book to all young scientists, wherever they are, but especially to two microscientists, Noah and Kay, our beloved grandsons.

- Ron Pickering

Contents

Introduction

About this book

Science for Common Entrance: Biology covers the Biology component of Science at Key Stage 3 and is part of an ISEB-approved course leading to 13+ Common Entrance.

In this book you will continue your exploration and investigations into the lives of plants and animals, starting with the basic unit of all life; cells. You will explore in more detail the life processes of nutrition, respiration and reproduction. You will learn something about the ways in which different living organisms, including ourselves, all depend on one another for survival; and about how different organisms get their differences, and how they are passed on from generation to generation.

The book is part of a *Science for Common Entrance* series, which also includes *Chemistry* and *Physics*.

- *Chemistry*: This is where you will find out about the properties of different materials. You will see that many of these properties are explained by the fact that materials are made of tiny particles.
- *Physics*: In this book you will study the physical processes that affect your everyday life. The book will explain forces, electricity and magnetism, and the properties of light rays and sound waves.

Of course, scientists from the different areas of science work together so don't be surprised if you are asked to think about some Chemistry as you study Biology or some Physics as you study Chemistry!

What do we mean by science?

As you go through this book you will continue to build on the scientific knowledge you have already gained. Remember that asking questions about the world around you is the first step to becoming a scientist. Carrying out experiments is a good way for scientists to start finding things out and to begin to answer some of the more challenging questions we have. You will already have got to grips with the idea of conducting fair tests when carrying out experiments and in this book we will give you the opportunity to do many more. You will also see some of the things we have found out from the results of experiments carried out by other scientists.

◯ Notes on features in this book

Words printed in blue bold are keywords. All keywords are defined in the Glossary at the end of the book.

Sometimes you will see the heading **'Preliminary knowledge'**. The material in these sections is a reminder of information you should have learned at primary school. If any of this material is not familiar take time to ask your teacher or read about the subject in books or online, before moving on.

> Useful rules and reminders and additional notes, looking like this, are scattered throughout the book.

Did you know?

In these boxes you will learn interesting and often surprising facts about the natural world to inform your understanding of each topic. Sometimes you will find a brief biography of an important scientist. You are **not** expected to learn these facts for your exam.

Working scientifically is an important part of learning science. When you see this heading you will be reading about the skills and attitudes you need to be a good scientist. You will find out:

Working Scientifically

- why we carry out experiments
- how to plan and carry out experiments
- how to evaluate risks
- how we ensure our findings are accurate and precise
- what we mean by the word 'variable'
- how to identify the independent, dependent and control variables
- how we measure variables
- what we mean by a fair test
- how to properly record and display results and observations
- how to spot patterns and draw conclusions
- how to calculate results, analyse data and use simple statistical techniques
- how scientific methods and theories develop as scientists modify explanations to take into account new evidence and ideas
- about the power and limitations of science and potential ethical issues.

Investigation

When we think like a scientist we might try to give some sort of explanation for what we observe. For example, we might think that some mice are bigger than others because of what they eat.

In an investigation you will see a brief overview of how to carry out an experiment and how to record and interpret your observations, to check out an explanation. Sometimes sample data is provided so that you can practise data analysis techniques, presenting data in graphs and charts and interpreting the results and drawing conclusions.

The investigations given in this book are **not** intended as step-by-step instructions – your teacher or technician should provide these and carry out their own risk assessment if you are to carry out the investigation in the classroom. Do **not** try any of these investigations outside of the classroom without teacher supervision.

Exercise

Exercises of varying lengths are provided to give you plenty of opportunities to practise what you have learned. Answers are provided in the separate resource, *Science for Common Entrance: Biology Answers*.

Go further

When you see this heading, this highlights information that is beyond the requirements of the ISEB 13+ Common Entrance exam. You therefore do not need to remember the detail of this information for your exam, but it is helpful to understand the principles and applications of science described, in order to fully support your understanding of the subject area.

⃝ What is biology?

Scientists believe that the Earth was formed from an enormous cloud of gases about 4 600 000 000 (4.6 billion) years ago. Conditions were harsh – there was no oxygen gas and the environment was very unstable. It is thought that there might have been rainstorms that lasted for hundreds of years and erupting volcanoes that could have caused tremendous temperature changes in some areas and certainly would have released great clouds of suffocating gases. Conditions were clearly very unsuitable for life as we know it!

Many scientists also believe that the first and simplest living organisms appeared on the Earth about 3 800 000 000 (3.8 billion) years ago. These first simple organisms probably fed themselves from chemicals present in a sort of 'soup' (sometimes called the primordial soup) that made up some of the shallow seas on Earth at that time.

Since the appearance of the first living organisms, a vast number of different types of organism (species) have evolved on Earth. Many have become extinct over the passage of time, for example dinosaurs, which became extinct around 65 million years ago. Scientists estimate that there are currently around 8–9 million different species on Earth, however only around 1.2 million have been identified.

Biology is the science of life. It is the study of living organisms. Biologists study their structure, function, growth, origin, evolution and distribution. The study of biology is the basis for many important scientific fields, including medicine, agriculture and environmental management. Many important advances in science and medicine have been made possible by the understanding of biology. Antibiotics, stem cell therapy, *in vitro* fertilisation, artificial heart pacemakers, the selective breeding of animals and plants, would not exist without the research of biologists. The living world is diverse and only 14–15 per cent of species have been identified – far fewer have been studied in detail. There is still so much to learn from the study of biology.

> You will learn about the seven characteristics that define something as 'living' in Chapter 1.

Investigations in science

Before we launch into this book it is worth pausing and taking some time to go over some of the rules we need to follow in order that we can carry out experiments in a reliable way. These rules apply whether you are studying biology, chemistry or physics.

◯ What is an experiment?

Every day we make hundreds of observations; for example, 'that metal dustbin has rusted more than the other one', 'that car is moving faster than the other one', 'that sunflower is taller than the one next to it' or 'some of the pet mice are bigger than the others'.

When we think like a scientist we might try to give an *explanation* for some of these observations. We might think that some mice are bigger than others because of what they eat. We might think that one sunflower is taller than the one next to it because it is getting more sunshine. Before it is proven, we call this explanation a **hypothesis**.

An **experiment** is a way of collecting information to see whether our hypothesis is correct. Before a scientist begins an experiment, he or she will have a definite **purpose** or **aim**. The aim of an experiment is a way of stating carefully what you are trying to find out. For example, 'My aim is to investigate the effect of protein on the growth of mice'. Not just, 'Study changing the diet of mice'.

What about variables?

An experiment has the aim of investigating the effect of one factor (protein in the diet, for example) on another factor (such as weight). These factors can have different values and so are called **variables**. In our experiment we can change the **values** of these variables, so we might give one group of mice more protein than we give another group. Anything that we can measure is a variable.

The experiment must be a fair test

Here are the steps you should follow before conducting an experiment:

Step 1: Write down your hypothesis and identify the variables. (Variables are factors that might affect the results.)

Step 2: Choose which variable you will change. This is called the **independent (input) variable**.

Step 3: Choose the variable that you think will be affected by changing the input (independent) variable. This is called the **dependent (outcome) variable**.

Step 4: Decide what equipment you will need to measure any changes. Then go ahead and carry out your experiment.

You are trying to find out whether the change in the independent variable causes a change in the dependent variable.

An experiment will not be a **fair test** if you change more than one variable at a time. To make sure that the experiment is a fair test, you will need to check that none of the other possible variables is changing.

For example, in the experiment investigating the mass of mice, it is possible that the mass might be affected by any of the following factors:

- how old they are
- how much water they drink
- how much protein is in their diet
- other foods they eat
- how big their cage is.

These are the variables. If you want to investigate how protein affects the mass of mice, all of the other variables **must stay the same**. These are called the **control variables**.

Finally remember to **work safely**.

- Always wash your hands after touching plants or animals.
- Carry equipment carefully.
- Don't run in the laboratory.
- Wear suitable clothing.

◯ How we measure variables

Scientists often need special equipment to measure any changes in variables during the course of their experiments. Some of these pieces of equipment, and what you would use them for, are described here.

Measuring length using a ruler

A ruler can be made of wood, metal or plastic. Along the length of the ruler is a numbered scale. One of the benefits of a plastic ruler is that it is usually transparent, so the object to be measured can be seen through it. The following diagram reminds you how to use a ruler.

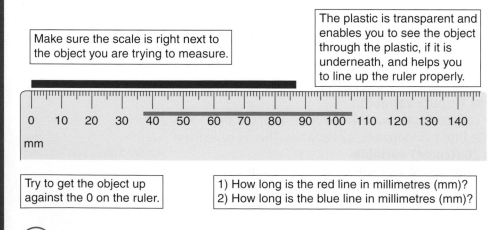

Make sure the scale is right next to the object you are trying to measure.

The plastic is transparent and enables you to see the object through the plastic, if it is underneath, and helps you to line up the ruler properly.

0   10   20   30   40   50   60   70   80   90   100   110   120   130   140

mm

Try to get the object up against the 0 on the ruler.

1) How long is the red line in millimetres (mm)?
2) How long is the blue line in millimetres (mm)?

Measuring volume using a beaker or a measuring cylinder

Beakers and **measuring cylinders** can be made out of glass or plastic. Scientists now often use plastic because it is less likely to break and so is safer. However, plastic beakers can't be used to boil liquids because they would melt and become distorted and useless.

The following diagram shows you how to use a measuring cylinder and a beaker.

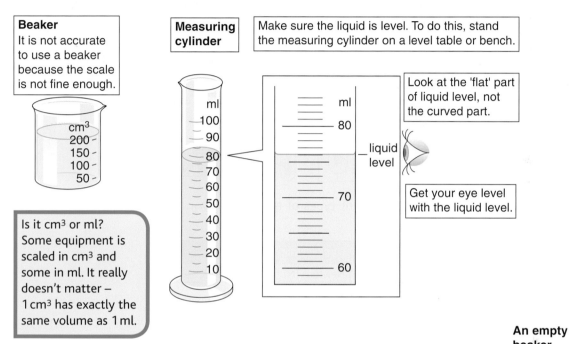

Beaker
It is not accurate to use a beaker because the scale is not fine enough.

cm³
200
150
100
50

Is it cm³ or ml? Some equipment is scaled in cm³ and some in ml. It really doesn't matter – 1 cm³ has exactly the same volume as 1 ml.

Measuring cylinder

Make sure the liquid is level. To do this, stand the measuring cylinder on a level table or bench.

ml
100
90
80
70
60
50
40
30
20
10

ml
80

liquid level

70

60

Look at the 'flat' part of liquid level, not the curved part.

Get your eye level with the liquid level.

Measuring other things

There are other things that scientists want to measure. These include temperature, force and mass. Measuring force is described in Physics, Chapter 3.

Measuring mass using a balance

Mass is the name given by scientists to the amount of a substance. You can use a **balance** (also called a **weighing machine**) to measure the mass of something. It is very important to remember that if you are weighing liquid in a container, you must subtract the weight of the container. You can do this as follows:

Step 1: Weigh the empty beaker. Note down its mass.
Step 2: Add the liquid and weigh the beaker again. Note down this mass.
Step 3: Subtract the mass of the empty beaker (Step 1) from the mass of the beaker containing liquid (Step 2).

An empty beaker

102.4g

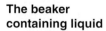

Balance
(weighing machine)

The beaker containing liquid

312.8g

Measuring temperature using a thermometer

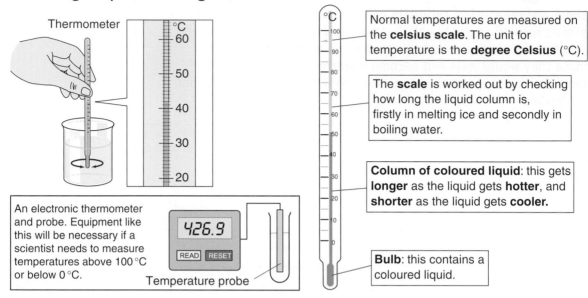

An electronic thermometer and probe. Equipment like this will be necessary if a scientist needs to measure temperatures above 100 °C or below 0 °C.

Temperature probe

Normal temperatures are measured on the **celsius scale**. The unit for temperature is the **degree Celsius** (°C).

The **scale** is worked out by checking how long the liquid column is, firstly in melting ice and secondly in boiling water.

Column of coloured liquid: this gets **longer** as the liquid gets **hotter**, and **shorter** as the liquid gets **cooler.**

Bulb: this contains a coloured liquid.

This table gives you a summary of different types of measuring equipment and their uses:

Equipment	What it measures	Units (symbol)
Forcemeter	Force (and weight)	Newtons (N)
Balance	Mass	Grams (g) and kilograms (kg) 1000 g = 1 kg
Stopwatch or stopclock (analogue or digital)	Time	Seconds (s) and minutes (min) 60 s = 1 min
Measuring cylinder or beaker	Volume	Millilitres (ml) and litres (l) 1000 ml = 1 l
Ruler/tape measure	Length	Millimetres (mm) and metres (m) 1000 mm = 1 m
Thermometer	Temperature	Degrees Celsius (°C)

Exercise 1: Made to measure

1 Give two reasons why glass and plastic are useful materials.
2 Choose the best reason why glass is more useful than plastic when making measuring equipment for use in Biology.
   A. Glass is cheaper
   B. glass can be cleaned by boiling it in water
   C. glass is less likely to break
   D. it is easier to put markings on glass
3 Choose the best reason why plastic is more useful than glass when making a ruler for measuring biological specimens.
   A. plastic is clearer than glass
   B. plastic is always cheaper
   C. plastic is less likely to break and damage specimens
   D. plastic is less shiny so markings are easier to read

Extension questions

4 Look at this diagram. A scientist has measured the mass and the volume of some water.

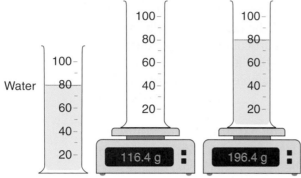

We know that about 70 per cent of a human body is made up of water.
The average weight of a class of 11-year-old students is 50kg.
Calculate the volume of water in the body of one of these students .

5 Minnie is going on a trip and she wants to take some water. She has a water container that weighs 120g. She doesn't want to carry more than 260g altogether.
   (a) What is the maximum mass of water she should take with her?
   (b) Minnie is an average 11-year-old in terms of body weight. She needs to replace about 5 per cent of her body water on this trip. Will she have enough water with her ?
   (c) Suggest two ways that Minnie would lose water from her body.

◯ Making a record of our results

Results (or **observations**) are a record of the measurements you have taken during an experiment. There are certain rules about the way you should show these results. They should be recorded in a table, like the one shown below.

Use a ruler to draw lines around your table. It makes it look **neater** and **more scientific!**

Give the columns headings by putting the name of the variable **and** the units.

In the first (left-hand) column, put the values for the **independent variable**, e.g. the amount of protein in the food.

In the right-hand columns, put the values for the **dependent variable**, e.g. mass of mice for each test.

Write the values as **decimals** not as **fractions**, e.g. 6.5 **not** 6½.

Calculate the mean (average) and put this in the last column.

Amount of protein in food, in grams	Mass of mice, in grams			
	Test 1	Test 2	Test 3	Mean
2	50	52	54	52
4	55	54	53	54
6	56	57	55	56
8	58	58	58	58
10	59	60	61	60
12	62	60	61	61

Put the numbers in order, not just mixed up. For example, 2, 4, 6, 8, 10 rather than 2, 10, 6, 8, 4. If you do, it makes it much easier to see patterns in your results.

When you look at your results, you may see a certain pattern. It might seem, for example, that the more protein a mouse gets in its diet, the faster it grows.

Your results will be more reliable if you carry out each test more than once and then take an **average** (mean) of the results. This will remove any unusual results from, for example, a particularly greedy mouse.

The mean is calculated by adding together all your results and dividing by the number of repeats. For example, the mean of 52, 50 and 48 is: $\dfrac{(52 + 50 + 48)}{3} = 50$

If one or two of the results don't fit the pattern, the first thing to do is check your measurement. If your measurement was accurate, and you have the time, you can **repeat** the test to check the 'odd' result.

Displaying your results

Sometimes you can see a pattern in your results from the table you have made, but this is not always the case. It often helps to present your results in a different way. **Charts** and **graphs** display your results like pictures and they can make it very easy to see patterns, but only if they are drawn in the correct way. There are rules for drawing graphs and charts, just as there are rules for putting results into tables.

● First of all, look at the variables you measured. If both of the variables have numbers as their values, you should draw (sometimes we say 'plot') a **line graph**. If one of the variables isn't measured in numbers, you should choose a **bar chart**.
● You should always put the **independent (input) variable** on the **horizontal** (x) axis and the **dependent (outcome) variable** on the **vertical** (y) axis. If you don't do this, you can easily mix up the patterns between the two variables.

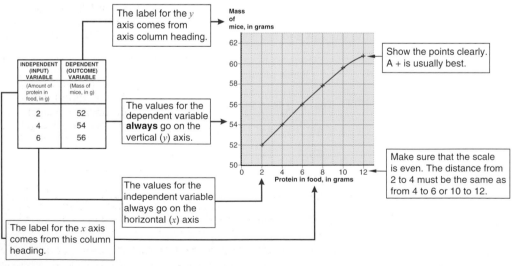

■ How to draw a line graph

The title should be: 'The effect of the amount of protein in their food on the mass of the mice'. The simple rule is: 'Effect of (independent variable) on (dependent variable)'.

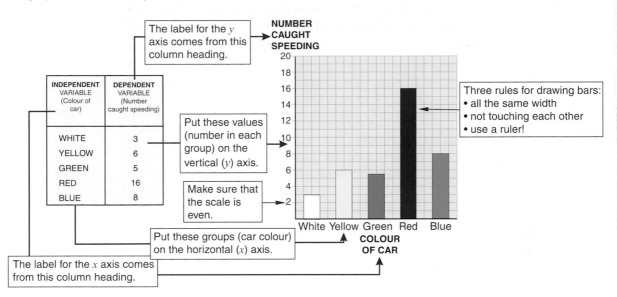

The label for the *y* axis comes from this column heading.

NUMBER CAUGHT SPEEDING

INDEPENDENT VARIABLE (Colour of car)	DEPENDENT VARIABLE (Number caught speeding)
WHITE	3
YELLOW	6
GREEN	5
RED	16
BLUE	8

Put these values (number in each group) on the vertical (*y*) axis.

Three rules for drawing bars:
• all the same width
• not touching each other
• use a ruler!

Make sure that the scale is even.

Put these groups (car colour) on the horizontal (*x*) axis.

COLOUR OF CAR

The label for the *x* axis comes from this column heading.

■ How to draw a bar chart

In this case the title should be 'The effect of the colour of the car on the number caught speeding.

Using graphs

A graph can let you see a pattern between two variables. For example, as protein in their diet increases, so does the mass of the mice. The graph can also let you make **predictions** if it shows an obvious pattern. So, you might be able to predict how much a mouse would weigh if it were fed on a diet containing a certain amount of protein.

Just before we look at how to do this using a graph, it is worth making an important point about predictions. It can be very useful indeed to make some of your own predictions even *before* you get started on your experiment. If you do this, it can help you to plan much better experiments. If we take the example of looking at the effect protein has on the mass of the mice eating it, we can make a pretty good guess (a prediction) that

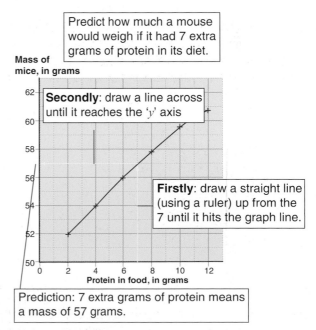

Predict how much a mouse would weigh if it had 7 extra grams of protein in its diet.

Mass of mice, in grams

Secondly: draw a line across until it reaches the '*y*' axis

Firstly: draw a straight line (using a ruler) up from the 7 until it hits the graph line.

Protein in food, in grams

Prediction: 7 extra grams of protein means a mass of 57 grams.

the more we feed them, the heavier the mice are likely to become. We can also start to plan what apparatus we will need and so on.

Making conclusions

Once you have collected all of your results into a table, and perhaps drawn a graph or chart, you need to sum up what you have found out. This summing up is called a **conclusion**, and here are some tips:

- **Your conclusion should be related to the aim of your experiment.** If your aim was to investigate the effect of light intensity on plant growth and you saw a clear pattern, then your conclusion might be that 'the higher the light intensity, the taller the plant'.
- **Try to write your conclusion simply.** One sentence is often enough, but make sure it explains how the independent (input) variable affects the dependent (outcome) variable for your experiment.
- **Don't just describe your results.** For example, in the experiment on mouse growth the statement 'a lot of protein in the diet makes a mouse heavy' is really giving only one of your results. A much better conclusion would be 'the greater the amount of protein in the diet, the heavier the mouse becomes'.

Cells and organisation

Everyone has some ideas about what living things do. Birds fly, horses run, fish swim and plants bend towards light. Most living things get taller, heavier and wider. They all seem to produce seeds or eggs, or give birth to live young. On the other hand, bricks, steel girders, car tyres and pieces of furniture do not do any of these things and so we say that they are non-living.

Deciding whether something is living or non-living is not always so clear cut. For example, is a dried-out seed or a virus particle living or non-living? To try to answer this type of question it is useful to make a list of characteristics that we might expect living organisms to have.

The seven processes: the characteristics of life

All living organisms carry out these seven life processes (see the diagram on the next page):

- **respiration**
- sensitivity (they respond to their environment)
- movement
- nutrition (they nourish themselves)
- **growth** (they grow and develop)
- excretion
- reproduction.

Living organisms are made of cells

A living organism is made up of many different chemicals. Even the simplest living organisms have chemicals arranged into units called **cells**. The cell is the basic unit of all living things.

Although cells exist in a number of types and forms and may take on very specialised functions, they have common features that can be recognised in almost all of them.

Each cell, whether it comes from a plant or an animal, has:

- a **cell-surface membrane**, which surrounds the cell and separates it from its environment
- **cytoplasm**, which provides the environment for most of the work of the cell, including respiration in mitochondria

> Without **energy** a living organism cannot carry out its life processes. When scientists check Mars for signs of life, they look to see whether there is anything there that can carry out the process of **respiration**.

- a **nucleus**, which contains genes made up of DNA. The DNA contains coded information to make specific proteins. These are key in controlling the activities of the cell. DNA also determines a cell's and/or an organism's characteristics.

Most animal and plant cells also have mitochondria, small structures that can release energy from food.

In addition, **plant cells:**

- are surrounded by a **cellulose cell wall**
- often contain a permanent fluid-filled **vacuole**
- may have chloroplasts within the cytoplasm.

Respiration: This is the process which releases energy from food. Plants and animals need energy for movement, growth and repair. Respiration usually needs oxygen (see Chapter 4) and can be summarised by this simple equation:

glucose + oxygen ⟶ carbon dioxide + water + energy

Movement: Animals use energy to move around in search of food, water, warmth and safety. Most plants are fixed by their roots. They move towards light, water and nutrients by growth. This is much slower than animal movement.

Growth: Plants and animals grow from a single cell until they are adults. Animals usually stop growing at this stage but trees and other plants can keep growing until they cannot get enough nutrients from their surroundings (see Chapter 5).

Excretion: Nutrition and other processes produce waste material that cannot be used. Animals get rid of waste gases from their lungs. The kidneys keep the body free from impurities; they remove excess water from the blood and create a waste liquid called urine. Animals also excrete dissolved waste in sweat. Unused solid material is removed (**egested**) as faeces. Plants accumulate waste products in their leaves. These are excreted when the leaves fall from the plant.

Nutrition: Plants and animals need food for energy and growth. Green plants make their own food from carbon dioxide and water by photosynthesis. Animals cannot make their own food so they eat organic food made by plants (see Chapter 3).

Sensitivity: All living things can sense and react to changes in the environment. Animals react to temperature, light, sound, smell, taste and physical stimuli, such as being jabbed with a pin! Plants react by growing towards light and away from gravity.

Reproduction: All living things can make new organisms like themselves. Simple organisms, such as bacteria, do this by splitting in half (**asexual reproduction**). Complex plants and animals reproduce **sexually** to produce fertilised eggs or seeds (see Chapters 5 and 6).

■ The seven processes of life

The *common features* of plant and animal cells allow these cells to carry out the basic processes necessary to remain alive. For example, within the cytoplasm the mitochondria are small structures that can release energy from food, and within the nucleus the DNA is arranged in a way which allows the cell to control its own activities.

The *differences* between plant and animal cells are due to the differences in lifestyle between animals and plants, especially in their different methods of nutrition. Plants make their own food by a process called photosynthesis (see Chapter 8); animals consume (eat) plants and/or other animals. The following diagram shows a comparison of typical animal and plant cells.

Animal cell

Plant cell

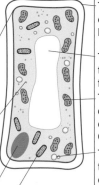

Common features of animal and plant cells

The **cell-surface membrane** surrounds the cytoplasm. It controls the entry and exit of dissolved substances and is responsible for separating the cell's contents from its surroundings.

The **cytoplasm** contains water and dissolved chemicals. Most of the chemical reactions, such as respiration, go on in the cytoplasm.

The **nucleus** contains the genetic material called **DNA**, which makes up genes and chromosomes. The DNA carries the coded instructions that control the activities and characteristics of the cell.

The **mitochondria** are structures that carry out the release of energy, by respiration, from glucose and oxygen.

Plant cell features

The **cellulose cell wall** is rigid (stiff) enough to support the cell but can let water and gases pass through.

The **large vacuole** helps to support the cell and can be used as a store for chemicals.

The **chloroplasts** contain the chlorophyll needed to absorb light energy for photosynthesis (see Chapter 7).

The **starch storage granules** show that photosynthesis has been going on.

■ A typical plant cell. Special plant cell features often relate to photosynthesis (see Chapter 7)

■ A typical animal cell. Plant and animal cells have common features that relate to carrying out life processes

Did you know?

As well as animal and plant cells, there is another, simpler type of cell belonging to bacteria. Bacterial cells are smaller than animal and plant cells and do not have a nucleus; instead they contain free DNA in their cytoplasm. They do have a cell-surface membrane, which is surrounded by a cell wall.

You will have heard of bacteria – these are single-celled organisms, some of which are responsible for bacterial diseases. You will learn more about bacterial diseases in Chapter 6, and will encounter other 'useful' types of bacteria as you progress through this book.

The size of cells

Most animal cells are quite small. In fact, you could fit 40 to 50 of them into a 1mm circle. Plant cells are bigger. You could only fit about ten of them into a 1mm circle. Both types of cell (plant and animal) are too small to be seen with your unaided eye. You need to use a microscope to see them (see later in this chapter).

Large organisms are always **multicellular**; that is, they are made up of many cells. Different types of cell develop to carry out different tasks and functions – they become *specialised*. Some examples of cell **specialisation**, and the jobs that they carry out, are shown below.

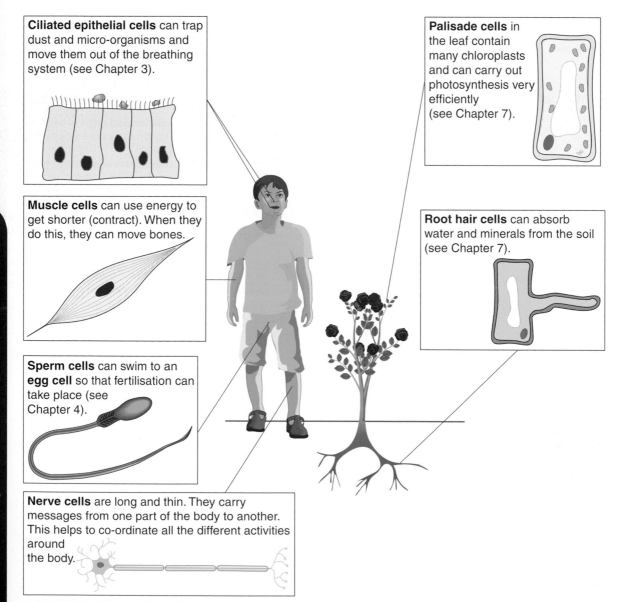

Ciliated epithelial cells can trap dust and micro-organisms and move them out of the breathing system (see Chapter 3).

Muscle cells can use energy to get shorter (contract). When they do this, they can move bones.

Sperm cells can swim to an **egg cell** so that fertilisation can take place (see Chapter 4).

Nerve cells are long and thin. They carry messages from one part of the body to another. This helps to co-ordinate all the different activities around the body.

Palisade cells in the leaf contain many chloroplasts and can carry out photosynthesis very efficiently (see Chapter 7).

Root hair cells can absorb water and minerals from the soil (see Chapter 7).

■ Specialised cells are adapted to carry out one task very efficiently

Preliminary knowledge: Human organs

Here is a reminder of the names, and positions of some of the organs of the human body. The functions and roles of these organs are also summarised.

The *lungs* are necessary to keep the correct balance of gases in the body **(gas exchange)**:
• they take oxygen from the air and put it in the blood
• they take carbon dioxide from the blood and put it back into the air.

The *liver* is necessary to complete the process of **nutrition**:
• it acts like a chemical factory
• it helps to deal with food taken in by the intestines
• it can store some useful parts of the food
• it makes a lot of heat which helps to keep the body warm.

The *kidneys* are necessary to keep the body free of impurities:
• they remove excess water from the blood
• they filter out impurities made by the body
• they make a waste liquid called urine
• the removal of waste products form the body is called **excretion**.

The *intestines* are necessary for the process of **nutrition**:
• they consist of a long tube,running from the mouth to the anus
• they break the food down so that useful substances can be taken into the blood.

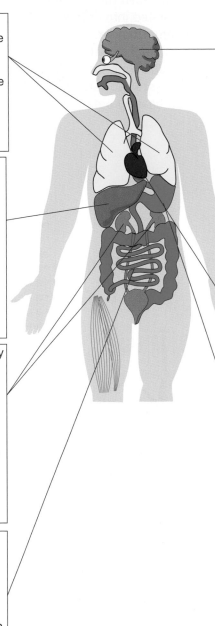

The *brain* is necessary for **control** of many **life process**:
• it helps us to decide what to eat
• it helps to control how quickly we grow
• it helps to tell us when to reproduce
• it can send messages to set off a set of movements
• receives messages from the sense organs
• nerves from the brain reach the rest of the body via the *spinal cord*.

The *heart* plays an important part in **nutrition** and **gas exchange**:
• it pumps blood through all of the parts of the body – the blood carries food from the intestines and oxygen from the lungs, to wherever it is needed.

The *stomach* plays an important part in **nutrition**:
• it stores food so that we don't have to eat all of the time!
• it churns up food and mixes it with chemicals that help to break the food down.

■ Some important organs of the human body

Cells, tissues and organ systems

Cells that have similar structure and function are joined together into **tissues**, and several tissues may be combined to form an **organ**. An organ is a complex structure with a particular function. When the different jobs needed to keep a whole organism alive are separated into different cells, tissues and organs, we say that there is **division of labour**.

Multicellular plants and animals contain many different types of cell. Each type of cell is designed for a particular function. Cells are organised to form tissues, organs and **organ systems**. Various organ systems together make up an **organism**. In a healthy organism, all systems work together.

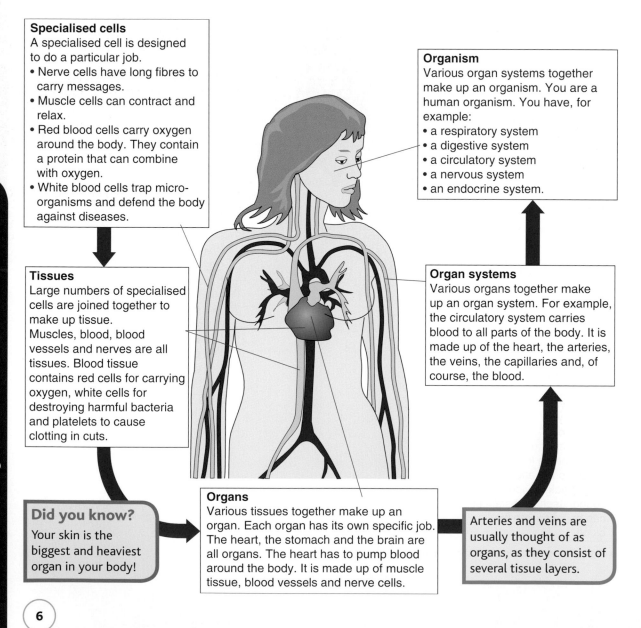

Specialised cells
A specialised cell is designed to do a particular job.
• Nerve cells have long fibres to carry messages.
• Muscle cells can contract and relax.
• Red blood cells carry oxygen around the body. They contain a protein that can combine with oxygen.
• White blood cells trap micro-organisms and defend the body against diseases.

Organism
Various organ systems together make up an organism. You are a human organism. You have, for example:
• a respiratory system
• a digestive system
• a circulatory system
• a nervous system
• an endocrine system.

Tissues
Large numbers of specialised cells are joined together to make up tissue.
Muscles, blood, blood vessels and nerves are all tissues. Blood tissue contains red cells for carrying oxygen, white cells for destroying harmful bacteria and platelets to cause clotting in cuts.

Organ systems
Various organs together make up an organ system. For example, the circulatory system carries blood to all parts of the body. It is made up of the heart, the arteries, the veins, the capillaries and, of course, the blood.

Did you know?
Your skin is the biggest and heaviest organ in your body!

Organs
Various tissues together make up an organ. Each organ has its own specific job. The heart, the stomach and the brain are all organs. The heart has to pump blood around the body. It is made up of muscle tissue, blood vessels and nerve cells.

Arteries and veins are usually thought of as organs, as they consist of several tissue layers.

In the most complex organisms, certain tasks may be carried out by several different organs working together. These organs all belong to a particular system.

Even though there is division of labour between different parts of the body, the efficient working of a complete living organism means that each part must be aware of what the other parts are doing and all their activities must be co-ordinated.

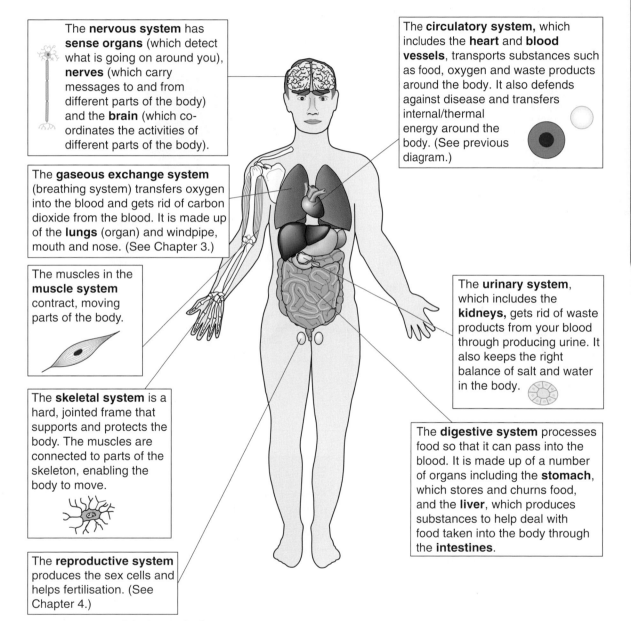

The **nervous system** has **sense organs** (which detect what is going on around you), **nerves** (which carry messages to and from different parts of the body) and the **brain** (which co-ordinates the activities of different parts of the body).

The **circulatory system,** which includes the **heart** and **blood vessels**, transports substances such as food, oxygen and waste products around the body. It also defends against disease and transfers internal/thermal energy around the body. (See previous diagram.)

The **gaseous exchange system** (breathing system) transfers oxygen into the blood and gets rid of carbon dioxide from the blood. It is made up of the **lungs** (organ) and windpipe, mouth and nose. (See Chapter 3.)

The muscles in the **muscle system** contract, moving parts of the body.

The **urinary system**, which includes the **kidneys,** gets rid of waste products from your blood through producing urine. It also keeps the right balance of salt and water in the body.

The **skeletal system** is a hard, jointed frame that supports and protects the body. The muscles are connected to parts of the skeleton, enabling the body to move.

The **digestive system** processes food so that it can pass into the blood. It is made up of a number of organs including the **stomach**, which stores and churns food, and the **liver**, which produces substances to help deal with food taken into the body through the **intestines**.

The **reproductive system** produces the sex cells and helps fertilisation. (See Chapter 4.)

■ Organ systems of the human body

Plants are specialised too!

It is important to remember that plants are living organisms. Although their **development** is different from animal development, they still follow the pathway from a single cell to the complex structure we recognise as a plant.

The plant body also contains many specialised structures capable of carrying out the life processes. The organ for gaseous exchange and photosynthesis in plants is the leaf, which is made up of different cell and tissue types, specialised to carry out specific functions.

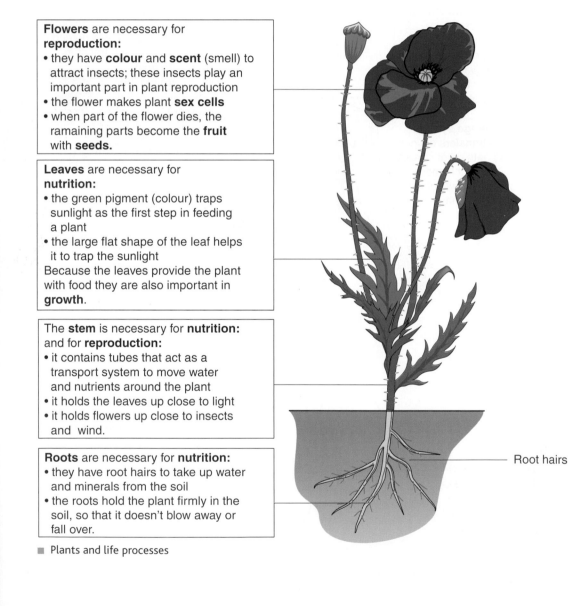

Flowers are necessary for **reproduction:**
- they have **colour** and **scent** (smell) to attract insects; these insects play an important part in plant reproduction
- the flower makes plant **sex cells**
- when part of the flower dies, the ramaining parts become the **fruit** with **seeds.**

Leaves are necessary for **nutrition:**
- the green pigment (colour) traps sunlight as the first step in feeding a plant
- the large flat shape of the leaf helps it to trap the sunlight

Because the leaves provide the plant with food they are also important in **growth**.

The **stem** is necessary for **nutrition:** and for **reproduction:**
- it contains tubes that act as a transport system to move water and nutrients around the plant
- it holds the leaves up close to light
- it holds flowers up close to insects and wind.

Roots are necessary for **nutrition:**
- they have root hairs to take up water and minerals from the soil
- the roots hold the plant firmly in the soil, so that it doesn't blow away or fall over.

Root hairs

■ Plants and life processes

Go further

Where do all the cells come from?

You began life as a single cell. This single cell is called a zygote (fertilised egg cell, see Chapter 4). You are now made up of millions and millions of cells and the amazing thing is that every one of them came from that original zygote. The zygote cell was copied over and over again by a process called **cell division**.

Growth depends on cell division

A fertilised egg cell (zygote) divides to make two **daughter** cells, which are identical. These divide to make four identical cells, which divide again and again to make a ball of cells called an embryo.

A fertilised egg cell divides to make two **daughter** cells, which are identical.

These divide to make **four** identical cells that divide again and again to make a ball of cells.

   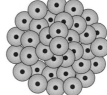

> #### Did you know?
>
> Because every division doubles the number of cells, it only takes about 40–60 divisions to go from a fertilised egg to a fully-formed human fetus.

At the same time as the cells were dividing to provide more 'building blocks' for your body, different groups of cells were taking on the special functions described in the section on specialised cells earlier in this chapter. So it is a combination of **cell division** and **cell specialisation** that made that original fertilised egg into the complete organism known as 'you'.

    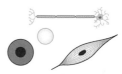

Fertilised egg (zygote)　　**Cell division**　　Ball of identical cells (embryo)　　**Cell division and specialisation**　　Specialised cells

What can go wrong?

Most cells can only divide a limited number of times. Once there are enough cells to carry out life processes, cell division should stop. Like other cellular processes, cell division is controlled by genes. If the cell division continues out of control, with cells growing and dividing, cancer can occur. Cancer results in the formation of cell masses or lumps called tumours. Tumours can prevent healthy tissues from working properly and can lead to death. Cancer can be due to:

- a mistake in the genes inside the nucleus
- something in the environment, such as tar in cigarette smoke, which damages the genes.

Go further

What about stem cells?

Some cells in the body do not become specialised straight away. They keep the ability to develop into almost any kind of specialised cell. They are called **stem cells**. Doctors and researchers believe that one day we may be able to grow new organs from stem cells. These organs could be used to replace damaged or diseased organs and so extend the life of very ill patients.

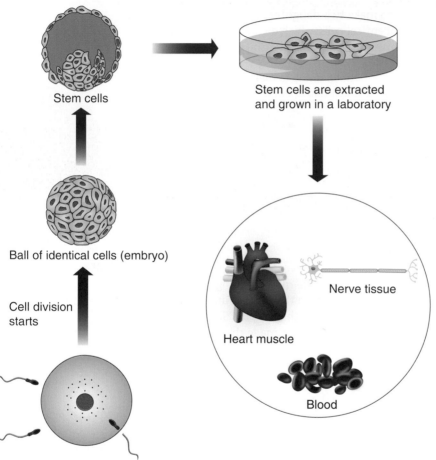

Stem cells

Stem cells are extracted and grown in a laboratory

Ball of identical cells (embryo)

Cell division starts

Nerve tissue

Heart muscle

Blood

Fertilised human egg (zygote)

■ Stem cell therapy – scientists are developing ways to use stem cells to repair or even replace damaged tissues and organs

Stem cells have been used in medicine for many years – bone marrow transplantation is a form of stem cell therapy. Ethical issues around stem cells mainly concern the use of embryonic stem cells. Embryos are considered the most scientifically valuable source of stem cells because these cells have the potential to become any type of body cell. In contrast, bone marrow stem cells, for example, can only become different types of blood cells.

Until recently, embryonic stem cells were obtained from embryos that were unwanted by-products of *in vitro* fertilisation (IVF) attempts; these could be voluntarily donated for use in research. In the UK, the law allows experimentation up to 14 days from conception. More recently, UK law was changed to allow researchers to create human embryos in the laboratory for use in research, using donated eggs and sperm.

The key difference here is that new human embryos are now being created specifically for research. Using either source of embryonic stem cells results in the destruction of the embryo and raises serious ethical concerns for many people.

Discuss with a partner what these concerns might be.

However, embryonic stem cells can be extremely valuable in medical research and treatment.

What is your view on the use of embryonic stem cells in science?

Exercise 1.1: Made for the job!

1 (a) From memory, draw a simple outline of a human body. Mark on it where you would find the brain, heart, lungs, stomach, intestines, liver and kidneys.

(b) Match up the words in the first column with the descriptions in the second column.

Stomach	Pumps blood around an animal's body
Heart	Remove impurities from the blood
Lungs	Controls many of the life processes in animals
Kidneys	Allow oxygen to enter the body
Brain	Stores and churns food
Liver	Deals with food taken into the body through the intestines

2 Match up the words in the first column with the descriptions in the second column.

Leaf	Make the plant's sex cells
Roots	Holds leaves up close to the light
Stem	Absorb minerals from the soil
Flowers	Traps sunlight

Microscopes

The light microscope

A human body consists of between 50 and 100 million million cells. These cells are too small to see with the unaided naked eye, so to study them clearly requires help. The instrument that is used to study cells is called a microscope.

- A microscope uses visible light to shine through a suitable **specimen**. A series of **lenses** then magnifies the image that is formed.
- The specimen, such as a sample of cells, is very thin, so it needs to be supported on a thin glass **slide**.

- The slide and specimen are transparent and allow the visible light to pass through to the magnifying lenses. The contrast of the image can be improved by using dyes or stains to pick out certain structures in the cell. The nucleus of an animal cell, for example, shows up particularly well when stained with a dye called **methylene blue.**
- A typical laboratory light microscope can give a useful magnification of about 400 times, which means the image the viewer sees is actually 400 times larger than the specimen. The maximum useful magnification of a sample with a light microscope is around 1500 times.

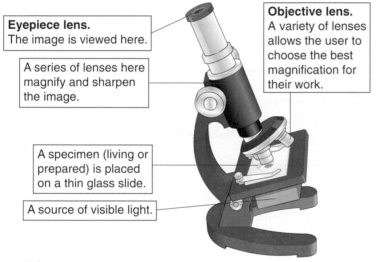

Eyepiece lens.
The image is viewed here.

A series of lenses here magnify and sharpen the image.

Objective lens.
A variety of lenses allows the user to choose the best magnification for their work.

A specimen (living or prepared) is placed on a thin glass slide.

A source of visible light.

■ A light microscope

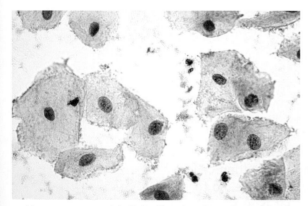

■ Here are some epithelial cells taken from the inside of a cheek, viewed using a light microscope. The nucleus (purple) shows up clearly using a stain. This sample has been magnified 1000 times.

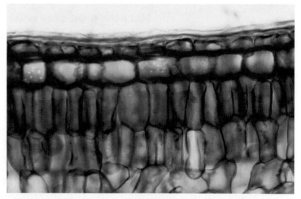

■ These are palisade cells in a holly leaf. They are the column-like cells beneath the top layer of the leaf. These cells have been viewed using a light microscope and magnified 240 times. A stain has been used on this sample that highlights the cell walls and nuclei.

Go further

The electron microscope

In the late 1930s a new kind of microscope was invented. This used a beam of electrons rather than visible light and was therefore called an **electron microscope**. The image shows up on a fluorescent screen. An electron microscope is much more powerful than a light microscope and can give a useful magnification of around half a million times! Enlarged to this extent, a single cell would cover an area the size of a football pitch. The maximum useful magnification of a sample with an electron microscope is around 2 million times.

> Electrons are negatively charged particles that surround atoms. All substances are made of atoms. You will learn more about atoms in Chemistry, Chapter 1 and about electrons in Physics, Chapter 9.

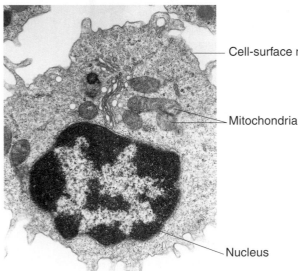

Cell-surface membrane

Mitochondria

Nucleus

■ This image captured with an electron microscope shows the increased detail that can be seen in an animal cell compared with a light microscope image. This sample has been magnified 11 250 times.

Since we need a microscope to see a cell, we might ask ourselves how big a cell actually is. If you look at the edge of a typical school ruler, it is likely that you will see it divided into millimetres (mm). A person with good eyesight can quite easily see an object that is one-tenth of a millimetre in length, but still cannot see an animal cell. A typical animal cell is about one-fiftieth of a millimetre in diameter. A typical plant cell is about one-tenth of a millimetre in diameter.

Tenths, twentieths and fiftieths are rather clumsy terms to use, so scientists more commonly use a system that deals with units of one thousand:

- one metre (m) contains one thousand millimetres (mm)
- one millimetre (mm) contains one thousand micrometres (μm).

A typical animal cell is about one-fiftieth of a millimetre in diameter, which is 20 μm (i.e. $\frac{1000}{50}$).

Investigation: Examining and recording cell structure

In this investigation you will use a light microscope to look at onion cells and make an accurate scientific drawing of your observations.

- Use a pipette to place a small drop of iodine solution onto a microscope slide.
- Cut out a small section – about 1 cm x 1 cm – from one layer of an onion (your teacher will show you how to do this).
- Use a pair of forceps to carefully remove the thin layer of cells from underneath this layer (your teacher will show you how to do this).
- Place the thin layer of cells flat (do not let it roll up into a ball) into the iodine solution. Leave it for two minutes so that the cells can stain.
- Now lower a cover slip onto the slide, as shown in the diagram. Do this slowly otherwise you will get air bubbles.

Cover slip

- Look at the cells under the microscope. Use low power first, then high power.
1 Make a drawing of a few of the cells. Label the cell wall, cytoplasm, cell-surface membrane and nucleus.
2 Using the high power lens, what is the magnification of the image you see?
3 What main difference in structure would you see if you were to examine human cheek cells?

Scientific drawings

When making scientific drawings from observations use a sharpened pencil and draw in clean lines – try not to sketch or shade. Your drawing should be two-dimensional. Label lines should be straight (drawn with a ruler), should not cross and they should not have arrow heads. Always add a scale bar or magnification and a heading that includes the source of the drawing, e.g. 'Onion cells observed under the light microscope'.

Opposite is an example of a good scientific drawing and beneath it, a bad one. What makes the upper image a good scientific drawing?

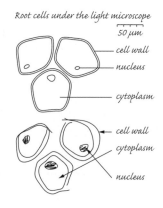

Root cells under the light microscope

50 μm
cell wall
nucleus

cytoplasm

cell wall
cytoplasm

nucleus

Investigation: Preparing slides of animal cells

In this investigation you will prepare a slide of your cheek cells, examine them under the light microscope and make an accurate scientific drawing of your observations.

- Use a cotton bud from a freshly opened pack. Your teacher will provide this. Gently scrape the inside lining of your cheek with one end of the cotton bud.
- Rub the end of the cotton bud over the centre of a microscope slide – you should see some cloudy material left on the slide.
- Immediately dispose of the cotton bud by placing it in a beaker of disinfectant. Your teacher will provide this.
- Add two small drops of methylene blue stain to the smear on the microscope slide. Leave the slide for two minutes to allow the cells to become stained.
- Now lower a cover slip onto the slide, as you did for the onion cells. Do this slowly otherwise you will get air bubbles under the slide.
- Look for cells under the microscope. Use the low power first to try to find some stained cells and then switch to high power to look at the cells in more detail.
1 Make a drawing of a few of the cells. Label the cell membrane, the nucleus and the cytoplasm.
2 Why do you think you have used methylene blue stain?

Exercise 1.2: Cells and tissues

1 This diagram shows a small group of cells from the root of a plant.

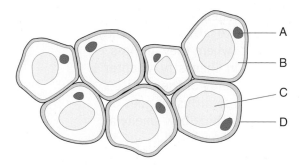

(a) Identify the parts labelled A, B, C and D.
(b) What do we call a group of similar cells with the same function?
(c) Your teacher gives you a very thin slice of a plant root. How would you get it ready for viewing under a microscope?
(d) Suggest two ways in which these cells are different from typical animal cells.
(e) Suggest one way in which these cells are different from typical leaf cells. Explain this difference.

2 Organs can carry out their functions because of the special cells they have. Rearrange the entries in this table to match up the cell with its function and process.

Cell	Function	Process
white blood cell	absorbs light	to prevent disease
leaf cell	transports oxygen	to digest food
cell in the intestine	traps micro-organisms	for photosynthesis
red blood cell	produces enzymes	for respiration

3 The diagram below shows a plant cell.

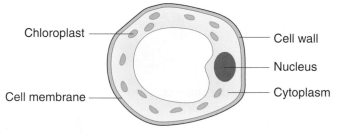

(a) Give the names of two parts of the cell, labelled on the diagram, which are not present in animal cells.

(b) State the function of each of the five parts of the cell labelled on the diagram.

Extension question

4 Use a library book or the Internet to find out any **disadvantages** of using an electron microscope.

Moving molecules: the process of diffusion

Particles such as molecules can spread out through liquids and gases, but not through solids. This spreading out is called **diffusion**. The particles spread out from where they are close together (where they are concentrated) to where they are far apart (where they are less concentrated). You will learn about diffusion in Chemistry, Chapter 1.

Diffusion depends on the kinetic (motion) energy of the particles (see Physics, Chapter 2). Heat supplies energy, so diffusion goes on much more quickly if the temperature is raised. Think how smelly a changing room is in summer compared with in the winter!

Diffusion takes place:

● whenever particles in gases or liquids mix
● from a high concentration to a lower concentration (i.e. down a concentration gradient)
● until the concentrations of the particles in the gases or liquids are the same.

Diffusion is the main process by which substances move over short distances in living organisms. Some of the life processes that involve diffusion are shown in the following diagram.

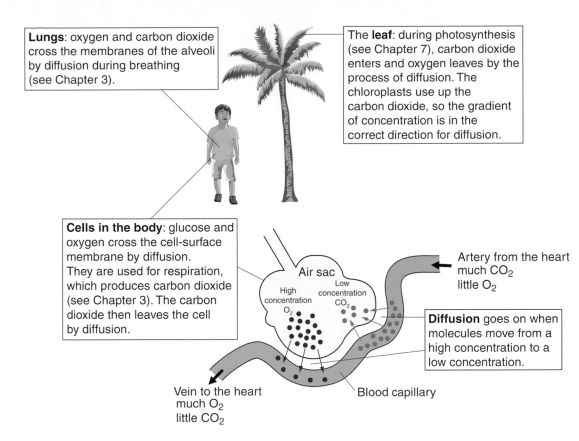

Lungs: oxygen and carbon dioxide cross the membranes of the alveoli by diffusion during breathing (see Chapter 3).

The **leaf**: during photosynthesis (see Chapter 7), carbon dioxide enters and oxygen leaves by the process of diffusion. The chloroplasts use up the carbon dioxide, so the gradient of concentration is in the correct direction for diffusion.

Cells in the body: glucose and oxygen cross the cell-surface membrane by diffusion. They are used for respiration, which produces carbon dioxide (see Chapter 3). The carbon dioxide then leaves the cell by diffusion.

Artery from the heart much CO_2 little O_2

Air sac

High concentration O_2

Low concentration CO_2

Diffusion goes on when molecules move from a high concentration to a low concentration.

Vein to the heart much O_2 little CO_2

Blood capillary

Unicellular organisms have structural adaptations

Multicellular organisms such as humans and plants have many adaptations of their tissues and organs. These adaptations allow the tissues and organs to perform their functions efficiently. However, it is not essential to be made of many cells to show adaptations for efficiency. Many **unicellular** (single-celled) organisms also show adaptations of structure to function.

Two examples of unicellular organisms are shown in the diagrams that follow. *Amoeba* move and feed by using bulges of cytoplasm. The *Euglena* can feed itself like a simple animal when food is available and like a plant if there is sufficient light!

Food vacuole: the membrane can form a sac to 'capture' small organisms such as bacteria. Once inside this sac, the *Amoeba* adds digestive enzymes to convert the food into soluble molecules. Some white blood cells carry out a similar process when defending the body against disease (see Chapter 7).

Cell-surface membrane: has a large surface area to allow diffusion of gases (oxygen into the cytoplasm and carbon dioxide out of it). The membrane is also flexible to help the *Amoeba* to move and to feed.

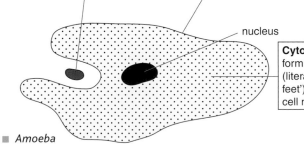

nucleus

Cytoplasm: can flow to form pseudopodia (literally means 'false feet') making the whole cell move forward.

■ *Amoeba*

Gullet: the cell can capture small food organisms and pass them into a feeding vacuole.

Cell-surface membrane: has a large surface area to allow diffusion of gases (oxygen into the cytoplasm and carbon dioxide out of it if no photosynthesis is going on). The membrane is not surrounded by a cellulose cell wall, but has a thin flexible covering.

Flagellum: the *Euglena* can use this to beat against the water and so move itself around. The red spot near the gullet helps the *Euglena* to work out which way to move.

Chloroplast: if the *Euglena* cannot catch enough food, it can use chloroplasts to feed itself by photosynthesis.

■ *Euglena*

Exercise 1.3: Unicellular organisms

1 Look carefully at the diagram of *Euglena*. Write down **two** ways in which it is *similar* to a typical plant cell and **three** ways in which it is *different* from a typical plant cell.

2 (a) Both *Amoeba* and *Euglena* are found in fresh water (such as slow-moving ditches and ponds). Suggest why they are only found in water.

  (b) Use the internet to find out how long these cells are. Make an outline diagram of each cell and add a scale line to represent 20 μm.

Nutrition

All living organisms require food to carry out the processes essential for life. They need this food to supply:

- the **substances** that will be the raw materials for growth and for repair of damaged parts of the body
- a **source of energy** to build these raw materials into cells and body parts
- **elements** and **compounds**, which are needed for the raw materials and energy to be used efficiently.

While *all* living organisms have these requirements, some organisms, the green plants for example, can make their own food substances by combining carbon dioxide gas from the air with water and nutrients from the soil (see Chapter 7). Other organisms *cannot* make their own food and must take in foods from their surroundings. Humans, like all other animals, are totally dependent on other organisms for their supply of food substances.

Preliminary knowledge: A balanced diet

The total of all of the food substances or nutrients a person takes in is called the **diet**. A healthy diet provides a human with the balanced selection of nutrients that it needs to carry out its life processes.

A **balanced diet** should contain the following seven food types: carbohydrates, proteins, fats, mineral salts, vitamins, water and fibre. Each is described in more detail on the next page.

Components of a balanced diet

Carbohydrates should supply most of the energy we need. They include **starches** and **sugars**, such as **glucose**. Starches are usually better than sugars because the body breaks them down more slowly, so we feel full for longer, and they do not cause problems such as tooth decay.

Carbohydrates should make up about 70% of the solid part of our diet; however, no more than 25% of this should be sugars. One chocolate bar and a single fizzy drink could easily contain the recommended maximum amount of sugar for a day. Examples of foods containing carbohydrates: bread, pasta, cereals, rice, biscuits, cakes, sweets.

Proteins are needed for the growth and repair of cells. We need proteins particularly while we are growing or when we are getting over an illness or injury. Pregnant women need to eat enough protein for themselves *and* for their growing baby. Examples of foods containing protein: fish, meat, milk, eggs, beans.

Fats supply energy. We can store lots of fat beneath our skin, where it acts as insulation and helps to keep us warm. Fats contain more energy than carbohydrates and we need to be careful that we do not eat too many fatty foods that might result in us putting on weight and may even cause damage to the heart and the circulation. There is a lot of fat in chips and crisps; even lean red meat has a lot of hidden fat. Full-cream milk, milk chocolate and ice cream also contain fat. Examples of foods containing fat: milk, cheese, butter, cooking oil, meat.

Minerals are substances that usually combine with another food to form parts of the body. For example, we need **calcium** (found in milk) to make strong teeth and bones and **iron** to produce red blood cells. Minerals are usually taken in with other foods, especially meats. Examples of foods containing minerals: meat such as liver, milk, vegetables.

Vitamins are substances that are needed in very small amounts, but are crucial for the body to be able to use other nutrients efficiently. There are many of them and they are usually taken in with other foods, especially dairy products. One of the most important is **vitamin C**. Citrus fruits such as oranges and lemons provide vitamin C. Without this vitamin we get bleeding gums and loose teeth and are more likely to catch a cold. Examples of foods containing vitamins: fruit, vegetables.

Water forms about 70% of the human body. Two-thirds of this water is in the cells, the other third is in blood. Humans lose about 1.5 litres of water each day in urine, faeces, exhaled air and sweat. This lost water must be replaced by water in the diet. We replace this water in two main ways: as a drink and in food, especially in salad foods like tomato and lettuce.

Dietary fibre is the indigestible component of food that comes largely from plant cell walls. It provides bulk for the faeces. As a result the muscles of the intestines are stretched and can push the food along. A shortage of fibre can cause constipation and may be a factor in the development of bowel cancer. Examples of foods containing fibre: wholegrain bread, cereals, fruit, vegetables.

Consequences of imbalances in the diet

If the diet does not provide all the nutrients in the correct proportions, the person may suffer from malnutrition. Some of the dangers of too much of a particular nutrient in the diet are shown in the following diagram.

High blood pressure: too much **salt** in the diet draws extra water into the blood. This can damage small blood vessels and may cause a stroke or heart attack.

Coronary heart disease: too much **fat** (including **cholesterol**) can block the blood vessels carrying oxygen to the heart.

Tooth decay: a diet with a high content of **sugary, acidic foods** can damage tooth enamel and dentine.

Obesity: too much 'energy' (usually too much sugar and fat) can cause a huge increase in **body mass**. This can lead to **heart disease, joint damage** and **diabetes**.

■ Dangers of an unbalanced diet

Too little can be just as bad as too much. If you have too little of a particular nutrient in your diet, you may develop a **deficiency disease** (see following diagram). If your body does not get enough food, **starvation** can occur.

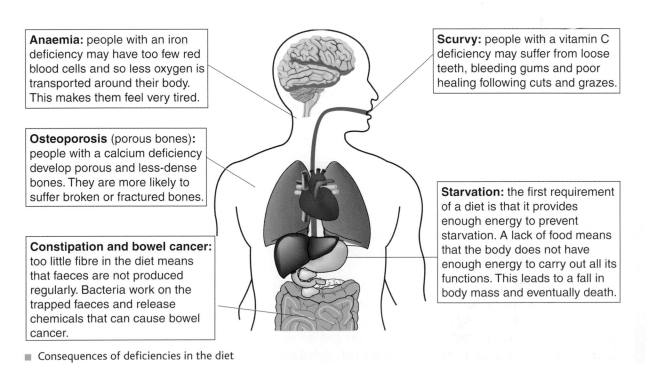

Anaemia: people with an iron deficiency may have too few red blood cells and so less oxygen is transported around their body. This makes them feel very tired.

Osteoporosis (porous bones): people with a calcium deficiency develop porous and less-dense bones. They are more likely to suffer broken or fractured bones.

Constipation and bowel cancer: too little fibre in the diet means that faeces are not produced regularly. Bacteria work on the trapped faeces and release chemicals that can cause bowel cancer.

Scurvy: people with a vitamin C deficiency may suffer from loose teeth, bleeding gums and poor healing following cuts and grazes.

Starvation: the first requirement of a diet is that it provides enough energy to prevent starvation. A lack of food means that the body does not have enough energy to carry out all its functions. This leads to a fall in body mass and eventually death.

■ Consequences of deficiencies in the diet

The following diagram shows the eatwell plate, produced by Public Health England. It can help you to achieve a balanced diet by showing the relative proportions of different foods you should choose to eat each day.

So, try to eat:

- plenty of fruit and vegetables
- plenty of bread, rice, potatoes, pasta and other starchy foods – choose wholegrain varieties whenever you can
- some milk and dairy foods
- some meat, fish, eggs, beans and other non-dairy sources of protein
- just a small amount of foods and drinks high in fat and/or sugar.

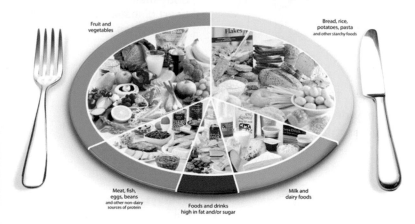

The eatwell plate © Crown copyright. Source: Public Health England in association with the Welsh government, the Scottish government and the Food Standards Agency in Northern Ireland.

Food tests

Testing foods for carbohydrates

Starch is an important food source for humans. It is made by plants and is contained in large amounts in potatoes, pasta and rice. There is a simple test for starch in food that is described in the following section.

Starch is made up of many glucose molecules. **Glucose** is a type of **sugar** and is a raw material for respiration. Because glucose can be obtained in our bodies by breaking down starch, we do not need much glucose in our diet. In fact, too much sugar can be very harmful, so it is important to be able to test a food for this substance.

Investigation: Testing food for starch and sugar

The aim of this investigation is to test different foods to see if they contain starch and/or sugar.

There is a simple test that can be used to tell us whether a certain food contains starch or not. This test uses a solution of iodine. The iodine solution gives a dark blue-black colour when it is mixed with a food containing starch.

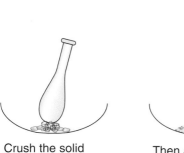

Crush the solid foods into small pieces.

Then add a few drops of iodine solution.

A blue-black colour means that the food contains starch.

Solution of food

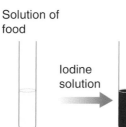

Iodine solution

You can test liquid foods too.

The simple test that is used to tell us whether a certain food contains sugar involves a chemical called **Benedict's solution**. The procedure is shown in the following diagrams.

Crush the food and dissolve it in water.

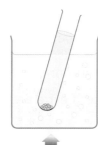

Add an equal volume of Benedict's solution.

Heat the mixture in a water bath (NOT over an open flame!).

Heat

A red–orange colour means that the food contains sugar.

Carry out these tests on a sample of different foods.

1 Draw a table like the one below to record your results.
   Use a tick to show the presence of a compound.

Food	Starch	Sugar

2 The test for sugar involves heating. State **two** steps that you should take
   to make sure that this heating is carried out safely.
3 Starch and sugar are both carbohydrates. We need carbohydrates in our diet
   to provide energy. Name the process that releases energy from carbohydrates.

◯ The energy requirements in the diet

Energy is required for all life processes. This energy is provided by
the process of **respiration**. This is a special chemical reaction (see
Chapter 3) that occurs in every living cell.

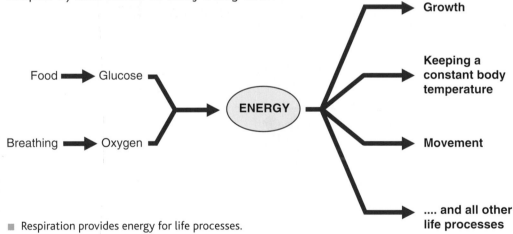

■ Respiration provides energy for life processes.

Respiration is such an important process that it must be carefully
controlled. Respiration is controlled by **enzymes** in cells.
   The amount of energy we require each day depends on:

● **age** – younger people are growing quickly and need extra energy to
  make new cells
● **gender** – boys usually need more energy than girls, as they are
  often more active with more muscle cells to use the energy
● **activity** – more movement requires more energy. People in
  'physical' jobs, such as building or road sweeping, need more
  energy than those in sedentary ('sitting down') jobs, such as
  office workers.

The important point to remember is that the **intake** of energy (from food) should approximately balance the **use** of energy (for life processes).

A food can be tested for its energy content (see Investigation: The energy content of food). Food packets must always show how much energy is present in the food. The amount of energy in a food is given in **joules** or kilojoules.

An **adequate diet** is one that provides enough kilojoules to drive all of the life processes. Starvation occurs when the body does not receive enough energy. The first priority in cases of famine is to provide enough energy, followed by the need to balance the diet. If the diet does not include enough energy-providing foods, the body will begin to break down its own tissues to release fats and carbohydrates. In the most extreme cases, the body will even break down protein (such as muscle) and the person will begin to waste away.

The opposite occurs when a person consumes a diet too high in energy. Excess energy is stored as fat tissue and the person will begin to gain weight, eventually resulting in obesity.

Working Scientifically

Investigation: Energy content of food

The aim of this investigation is to find and compare the energy content of different foods.

Food can be tested to find out its energy content. One way to do this is to burn a weighed sample of the food below a test tube containing water as show in the diagram:

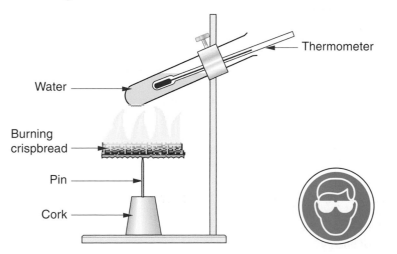

Energy from the burning food raises the temperature of the water in the test tube.

Your teacher will carry out a preliminary experiment with you to decide on the volume of water to use.

Before you start, make a **prediction** about which food sample contains the most energy and answer these questions:

1 What is the independent (input) variable for this experiment?
2 What is the dependent (outcome) variable for this experiment?
3 What factors must be kept the same for the test to be fair?

Design a suitable table to record the mass of your samples before burning, the temperature of the water before and after burning the food sample and the rise in temperature each time (which you will have to calculate).

You are now ready to carry out the experiment and record your results.

4 Was your prediction correct? Which of your foods appears to contain the most energy?
5 Can you think of ways in which your test might have been unfair? Were there any factors that might have influenced the temperature rise of the water that you couldn't do anything about?

Go further

Scientists who work in the food industry use a method of testing very similar to the one that you have carried out. They use the energy from burning food to heat water in a container. They have to be careful to make sure that almost all of the thermal energy from burning the food goes to the water. They then carry out a calculation to work out the energy that was in the food, knowing that it takes 4.2 J to make the temperature of 1 cm³ of water increase by 1 °C.

6 If a food sample raised the temperature of 10 cm³ of water by 80 °C, how much energy did the food sample give to the water?

Exercise 2.1: A balanced diet

1 A balanced diet consists of water and six other nutrients. What are these six other nutrients?

2 Match up the words in the first list with the functions in the second. Choose the *best* match in each case.

List 1:	List 2:
fish	can provide a lot of our water needs
butter	a good food for body-builders
spaghetti	a main source of energy
milk	a dairy product that can supply energy and some vitamins
wholemeal bread	helps prevent constipation
lettuce	excellent source of vitamins and minerals – an ideal baby food

3 The table shows the mass of water, fat, fibre and vitamin C in 100 g of potato. The potatoes have been cooked in three different ways.

	Water/grams	Fat/grams	Fibre/grams	Vitamin C/milligrams
100 g of chips	57	7	2	9
100 g of boiled, peeled potatoes	80	hardly any	1	6
100 g of potato baked in its skin	63	hardly any	3	14

(a) Use this information to help you copy and complete the following sentences.

(i) Chips are crisper than boiled potato because chips contain less _____.

(ii) Most of the fibre in a potato is in the _____ of the potato.

(b) Use the information in the table to work out how much vitamin C there is in:

(i) 200 g of chips: _____ mg

(ii) 200 g of potato baked in its skin: _____ mg.

(c) People do **not** always eat a balanced diet. Match the facts about a person's diet to the organ(s) it harms.

Fact about the diet
Not enough calcium
Not enough fibre
Too much fat

Organ harmed
Heart
Intestine
Bones

4 A student decides to burn a piece of crispbread to find out how much energy is stored in it (see the diagram on page 25). Energy from the burning crispbread raises the temperature of the water in the test tube.

Working Scientifically

(a) How should the student arrange the apparatus so that he is working safely?

(b) The student wants to find out whether potato crisps contain as much energy as crispbread. He does the experiment again using a piece of potato crisp. Suggest two things he must do to make the experiment a fair test.

The table shows some of the nutritional information from a packet of crispbread and a packet of potato crisps.

	Energy/kilojoules	Protein/grams	Carbohydrate/grams	Fat/grams	Fibre/grams
100 g of crispbread	1455	11.6	58.1	7.3	14.7
100 g of potato crisps	2072	5.8	57.9	28.7	4.3

(c) Using the apparatus shown earlier, the student burns 1.0 g of potato crisps. Which one of the results, **(i)** to **(iv) below**, will he get when he burns the potato crisps? Explain your choice.

   (i) The change in the temperature of the water will be greater.

   (ii) The change in the temperature of the water will be the same.

   (iii) The change in the temperature of the water will be smaller.

   (iv) There will be no change in the temperature of the water.

(d) (i) Fibre contains energy. Suggest why this energy cannot be used by the human body.

   (ii) Use the table to give two reasons for choosing crispbread rather than potato crisps as part of a balanced diet.

3 Respiration and gas exchange

Remember that living organisms need to carry out certain processes to remain alive. The most important of these life processes is **respiration**. This process provides the energy needed to carry out the other life processes.

⬭ What is respiration?

Respiration is a special kind of chemical reaction:

- It goes on in **every living cell** of every living organism. (Remember living organisms include micro-organisms and plants.)
- Glucose and oxygen react together to release energy in the **mitochondria** (see Chapter 1 – cell structure). Some of this energy is lost to the surroundings as thermal energy.
- Respiration produces two important chemical waste products – carbon dioxide and water.
- For animals with lungs, respiration depends on breathing, but it is important not to confuse these two processes. Respiration is *not the same as* breathing as we will see later in this chapter.

As with other chemical reactions, the process of respiration can be represented by a word equation:

$$\text{glucose + oxygen} \longrightarrow \text{carbon dioxide + water + energy}$$

$$\text{(Reactants)} \qquad\qquad \text{(Products)}$$

Because **oxygen** is required, this process is called **aerobic** respiration.

The reactants for respiration must be delivered to the cells in the bloodstream. The blood also takes away the waste products of this process. The supply of oxygen and the removal of carbon dioxide are made possible by the lungs, which provide an enormous surface area for these gases to move into or out of the blood. (See the section on 'lung structure' later in this chapter.)

Investigation: Checking on respiration

The aim of this investigation is to demonstrate that respiration is taking place. Because respiration produces carbon dioxide, water and energy, we can show that respiration is occurring if the amount of any of these products increases. The most reliable sign that respiration is taking place is the production of carbon dioxide.

Inhaled air · Breathing in · Breathing out · Exhaled air

Limewater – this solution turns cloudy when it reacts with carbon dioxide.

■ Testing for respiration

In this experiment your teacher will be passing inspired and expired air through a liquid called limewater.

Limewater is an **irritant**.

You must wear **safety goggles** when this experiment is being carried out.

When your teacher breathes in, air will bubble through the limewater on the way to his or her mouth. When he or she breathes out, the air will pass through the other tube of limewater.

Rubber tubing

Lime water

A   B

Record the results of what you saw in a copy of the table below.

	Before	After
Appearance of limewater in tube A (inspired air)		
Appearance of limewater in tube B (expired air)		

1   What can you conclude from the results?
2   What do these symbols mean?

Respiration without oxygen

Sometimes the blood cannot deliver oxygen quickly enough to the cells. This may happen when muscle cells are working hard during strenuous activity, for example. If no energy is available to the muscles, it can be disastrous. Breathing could be affected or an animal could be caught by a predator. Fortunately the body can continue to respire, at least for a short time, without the delivery of oxygen.

Respiration without oxygen is called **anaerobic respiration**. It does not occur in the mitochondria, but in the cytoplasm of the cell. In animals the word equation for anaerobic respiration is:

$$\text{glucose} \longrightarrow \text{lactic acid} + \text{some energy}$$

Anaerobic respiration has two drawbacks:

- It gives only about $\frac{1}{15}$ of the amount of energy per glucose molecule compared with aerobic respiration.
- Lactic acid, one of the products of the reaction, is poisonous. If it builds up, it stops the muscles from contracting. This can lead to fatigue and, eventually, death.

The harmful lactic acid is carried away in the blood and taken to the liver where it is oxidised. The body 'owes' itself some oxygen to do this. This extra oxygen (called an 'oxygen debt') is supplied by the deep, fast breathing that follows hard exercise.

Rest – all respiration is aerobic. Normal breathing and heart rates can supply the tissues with all the oxygen they need.

Glucose + oxygen → energy + carbon dioxide + water

Heart rate – 70 beats per minute

Breathing – 15 breaths per minute

Hard exercise – respiration is mainly anaerobic. Even though breathing and heart rate are high, the body still cannot provide the muscles with enough oxygen for aerobic respiration.

Glucose → energy + lactic acid

Heart rate – 140 beats per minute

Breathing – 50 breaths per minute

The muscles are getting energy without 'paying' for it with oxygen. They are running up an oxygen debt.

Recovery – paying off the oxygen debt. The breathing and heart rates remain high, even though the muscles are at rest. The extra oxygen is used to convert the lactic acid into carbon dioxide and water, paying off the oxygen debt.

Heart rate – 140 beats per minute falling to normal after some minutes

Breathing – 50 breaths per minute falling to normal after some minutes

Panting and rapid heartbeat continue until the lactic acid has been removed. Physically fit people recover more quickly.

■ The part played by aerobic and anaerobic respiration during rest, exercise and recovery

Products of anaerobic respiration in yeast and plants

In plants and yeast, lactic acid is not formed during anaerobic respiration. Instead the glucose is converted to carbon dioxide and ethanol by the following reaction:

glucose ⟶ carbon dioxide + ethanol + energy

In brewing and baking, where yeast is used, these products are very important. The carbon dioxide provides the 'bubbles' in some naturally fizzy drinks and makes dough rise into bread. The ethanol is, of course, the alcohol in alcoholic drinks.

> Preliminary knowledge: Anaerobic respiration is also important in other organisms.
>
> Yeast is a micro-organism that is too small to be seen with the naked eye. Yeast cells are important in the processes involved in making bread and wine.

Exercise 3.1: Respiration

1 The following drawing shows what happens to most of the energy that comes from the food that a hen eats in one day.

Food 1220 kJ

Waste 140 kJ

Egg 180 kJ

Movement and thermal energy 700 kJ

  (a) In the cells of the hen's body, energy is released from food by respiration. Copy and complete the word equation for this process:
  glucose + _____ → _____ + _____ + _____
  (b) (i) Calculate the total energy that remains in the body of the hen. What percentage of the total is this?
   (ii) What is this energy used for?

2 One of the comparisons between aerobic and anaerobic respiration shown in the following table is incorrect. Which one?

	Respiration	
	Aerobic	Anaerobic
A	Uses oxygen gas	Does not use oxygen gas
B	Produces ethanol or lactic acid	Produces no ethanol or lactic acid
C	Large amount of energy released	Small amount of energy produced
D	Mitochondria involved	Mitochondria not involved
E	Carbon dioxide always produced	Carbon dioxide sometimes produced

Respiration and breathing

> Remember:
>
> - Aerobic respiration uses oxygen to 'burn' (**oxidise**) food (glucose) and so releases the **energy** that cells need to stay alive (see Chapter 1 – characteristics of life).
> - Aerobic respiration produces **carbon dioxide** and **water vapour** as waste products.

$$\textbf{glucose + oxygen} \longrightarrow \textbf{carbon dioxide + water + energy}$$

Living organisms must be able to take oxygen *from* the air and get rid of carbon dioxide *to* the air. Swapping oxygen for carbon dioxide in this way is called **gas exchange**. This gas exchange takes place through a thin membrane at a gas exchange (or respiratory) surface.

Carbon dioxide is produced by respiration, it dissolves in blood plasma and is then brought to the lungs.

A gas exchange surface allows respiration to go on in cells

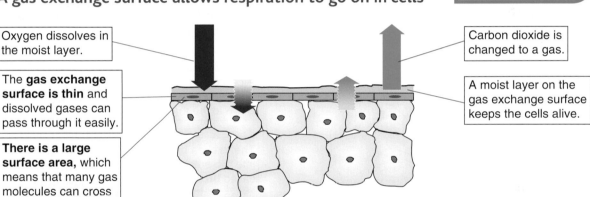

Oxygen dissolves in the moist layer.

The **gas exchange surface is thin** and dissolved gases can pass through it easily.

There is a large **surface area,** which means that many gas molecules can cross **at the same time**.

Carbon dioxide is changed to a gas.

A moist layer on the gas exchange surface keeps the cells alive.

Gas exchange is much more efficient if there is a method for delivering fresh supplies of air to this gas exchange surface. This method is called breathing. It is very important to remember the difference between breathing and respiration.

Breathing is the process that **moves air in and out of the lungs.**
Respiration is the process that **releases energy from food.**

It can be hard to remember this difference, since breathing is only needed because respiration takes place.

Gas exchange in humans

Humans are mammals, and like all other mammals they are active and keep a constant body temperature. Keeping a constant body temperature uses up a great deal of energy. The release of energy from respiration means that mammals must be able to gain oxygen and lose carbon dioxide. They must have a very efficient gas exchange system.

Preliminary knowledge: Lungs

The gas exchange system in humans is made up of the **lungs** and other tissues (it is an organ system). The lungs are located inside the ribs in the chest cavity.

The gaseous exchange system

Lungs provide a surface for exchanging oxygen and carbon dioxide. This surface is made up of the membranes lining the air sacs in the lungs.

Tubes from the mouth and nose carry air from the outside to the respiratory surfaces in the lungs. Once in the lungs, these tubes divide into many branches and this is sometimes called the **bronchial tree**. At the end of the narrowest tubes, the **bronchioles**, there is an air sac. These **air sacs** are made of a membrane that is so thin that the gases can diffuse across them very easily.

The lungs require a good blood supply (a special artery and vein) to carry dissolved gases to and from the respiratory surface. They also require a ventilation system (the intercostal muscles and the diaphragm) to keep a good flow of air over the respiratory surface.

The following diagram shows the arrangement of the parts of the human gas exchange system.

> If all the gas exchange surfaces in the lungs were spread out on the ground, the area would be around the same as that of a tennis court. To fit this huge structure into the chest, the lungs are **folded** many times to produce millions of tiny **air sacs**.

Air passing the **larynx** moves the vocal cords and helps us to speak. The larynx gets bigger at puberty in boys and is known as the 'Adam's Apple'.

Air passes into and out of the lungs through the **trachea** (windpipe). This tube is kept open by rings of cartilage.

Intercostal muscles are attached to the ribs.

Air enters through the nose and travels down to the throat.

The trachea branches into two smaller tubes called **bronchi.**

Each bronchus branches into many narrower tubes called **bronchioles.**

> Dust and micro-organisms in the air are trapped by special cells lining the trachea and bronchi. These cells make sticky **mucus** and have little hairs (cilia) that push the mucus back up out of the airways. It is either coughed up or passes into the gut instead.

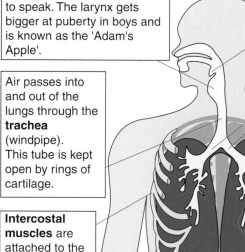
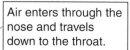

The diaphragm is a sheet of muscles that passes right across your body.

At the end of the bronchioles are **air sacs.** This is where oxygen moves **into** the blood and carbon dioxide moves **out**.

■ The human gas exchange system

Breathing ventilates the lungs

Take a deep breath and remember that:

- Living organisms must obtain oxygen *from* their environment and they must release carbon dioxide *to* their environment.
- An ideal gas exchange surface is thin, moist and with a large surface area.
- The human gaseous exchange system is made up of the lungs and the muscles that move them.
- Breathing is the set of muscular movements that keep the respiratory surface well supplied with oxygen (and, of course, remove carbon dioxide).

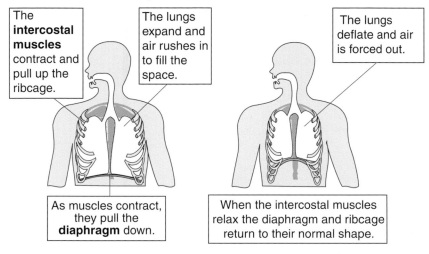

The **intercostal muscles** contract and pull up the ribcage.

The lungs expand and air rushes in to fill the space.

The lungs deflate and air is forced out.

As muscles contract, they pull the **diaphragm** down.

When the intercostal muscles relax the diaphragm and ribcage return to their normal shape.

Inspiration (inhalation)   **Expiration (exhalation)**

Measuring lung volume

Working Scientifically

It is possible to measure how efficient our breathing is. A doctor or a medical researcher can do this by getting a patient to breathe through a tube into a plastic chamber. The chamber is marked in measures of volume and so it is quite easy to measure:

- **tidal volume** – the amount of air breathed in and out with each normal breath
- **vital capacity** – the maximum amount of air that can be breathed in and out with the deepest breath the patient can manage.

These measurements provide information about how well the lungs are functioning in breathing. A normal male would expect to have a vital capacity of about 5000 cm^3 (females about 4000 cm^3), and both male and female would have a tidal volume of about 500 cm^3.

The capacity of the lungs can be increased by regular aerobic training, such as cross-country running or cycling. The effects of exercise on the heart and lungs are described in more detail in the section on healthy living in Chapter 6.

Investigation: How much air do you breathe out?

The aim of these experiments is to investigate how much air we breathe in and out.

Measuring vital capacity

- Fill a graduated plastic bottle with water and fit the lid.
- Fill a plastic washing up bowl no more than half full of water.
- Invert the bottle over the bowl and lower it until the lid is below the surface of the water.
- Remove the lid.
- Read the volume of water in the bottle and record this.
- Insert the rubber tubing into the mouth of the bottle.

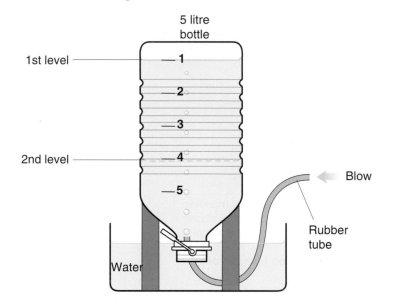

- Take a very deep breath and breathe out as much as possible through the tubing into the plastic bottle.
- Record the new volume of the water in the bottle.
1 Calculate your vital capacity. This is the difference between the two readings.
2 Heavy smokers usually have a reduced vital capacity. Suggest how this would affect their ability to exercise for long periods.
3 Even if you breathe out as deeply as possible, some air remains in the lungs. Suggest why this is important.

Measuring tidal volume

- Insert the tubing further into the bottle until it is above the surface of the water.
- Blow any water out of the tube.
- Support the bottle so that the water surface inside the bottle is level with the water in the bowl.
- Take a reading of the two levels as you breathe in and as you breathe out.

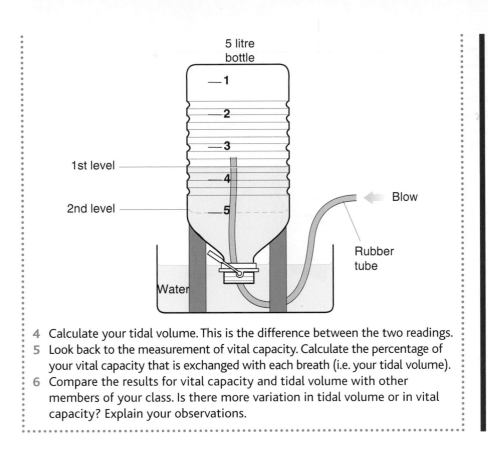

5 litre
bottle

1st level

2nd level

Blow

Rubber
tube

Water

4 Calculate your tidal volume. This is the difference between the two readings.
5 Look back to the measurement of vital capacity. Calculate the percentage of
  your vital capacity that is exchanged with each breath (i.e. your tidal volume).
6 Compare the results for vital capacity and tidal volume with other
  members of your class. Is there more variation in tidal volume or in vital
  capacity? Explain your observations.

Why do we need gas exchange?

All this breathing in and out ensures that oxygen can enter the blood
and carbon dioxide can be made to leave. If these changes did not
take place, there would be two unwanted results:

- Our cells would not get enough oxygen, which means they would
  not get enough energy from respiration and we would die.
- We would not be able to get rid of the waste carbon dioxide and
  we would poison
  ourselves. Carbon
  dioxide can turn
  our blood and other
  bodily fluids into a
  weak acid. This is
  another reason why
  we would die.

The diagram opposite
shows how the lungs are
able to exchange these
two gases between the
air and the blood.

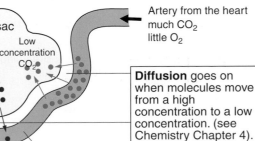

Artery from the heart
much CO_2
little O_2

Air sac
High
concentration
O_2
Low
concentration
CO_2

Diffusion goes on
when molecules move
from a high
concentration to a low
concentration. (see
Chemistry Chapter 4).

Blood capillary

Vein to the heart
much O_2
little CO_2

1 Rewrite the list of structures in order of size, with the smallest first.

trachea, air sac, bronchiole, bronchus

2 (a) The diagram on the right shows
         the lungs and the trachea, the
         airway leading to the lungs. One
         of the lungs is drawn in section. In
         the wall of the trachea there are
         pieces of a stiff material called
         cartilage. Suggest why is this stiff
         material necessary in the wall of
         the trachea?

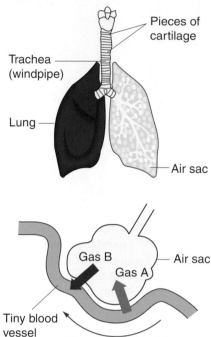

   (b) This diagram shows a single air
        sac and its blood supply.
        (i) Gas A enters the air sac from
             the blood. Gas B leaves the
             air sac and enters the blood.
             What are the names of
             gases A and B?
        (ii) Give one reason why it is easy
             for gases to pass across the
             wall of an air sac.

3 (a) What are the differences between
         the processes of breathing and
         respiration?
   (b) Why is breathing important?
   (c) Why is respiration important?
   (d) How would you check that respiration is taking place?

4 An athlete was trying to find out how much air he breathed out in one breath.
   He poured water into a bell jar and placed it upside down in a trough of water.
   The bell jar had a scale marked in cm^3. He breathed out one breath through
   the breathing tube. The result is shown in the right-hand diagram.
   (a) How much air did he breathe out?
   (b) Air contains carbon dioxide, nitrogen, noble gases, oxygen and water
        vapour. Give three differences between the composition of the air he
        breathed in and the air he breathed out.
   (c) State one other difference between the air breathed in and the air
        breathed out.

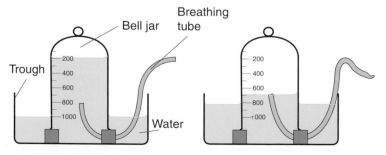

Extension question

5 Two schoolboys were asked to take part in an investigation into the effect of exercise on breathing. The number of breaths they took in each half minute was measured and recorded, first of all while sitting still, then when recovering from two minutes of hard exercise. The results are shown in the table.

Time/minutes	Activity	Number of breaths in each half minute	
		Tom	Alan
0.5	Sitting still	7	8
1.0	Sitting still	7	8
1.5	Sitting still	7	8
2.0	Exercise (step ups)	7	8
2.5	Exercise (step ups)		
3.0	Exercise (step ups)		
3.5	Exercise (step ups)		
4.0	Recovery (sitting)	25	25
4.5	Recovery (sitting)	24	24
5.0	Recovery (sitting)	23	17
5.5	Recovery (sitting)	18	13
6.0	Recovery (sitting)	15	10
6.5	Recovery (sitting)	12	10
7.0	Recovery (sitting)	12	9
7.5	Recovery (sitting)	10	8
8.0	Recovery (sitting)	8	8
8.5	Recovery (sitting)	8	8
9.0	Recovery (sitting)	7	8

(a) Draw a graph to show the changes in breathing rate over the time period of this investigation. Plot both lines on the same axes.

(b) Which boy appears to be fitter? Explain your answer.

Asthma

Asthma is a condition that makes breathing difficult, and an asthma sufferer may become very distressed. For a person suffering from asthma, air cannot easily move in and out of the lungs because:

- the muscles in the walls of the bronchi contract
- the lining of the bronchi 'leaks' a sticky mucus.

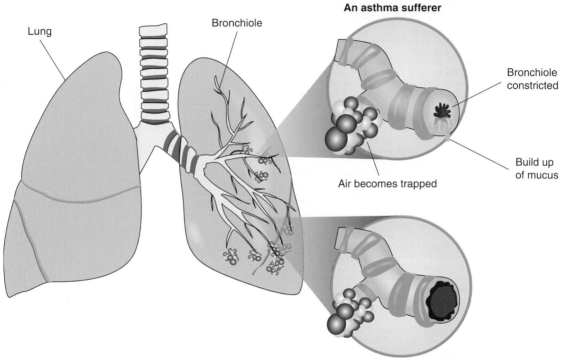

Lung

Bronchiole

An asthma sufferer

Bronchiole constricted

Air becomes trapped

Build up of mucus

A non-asthma sufferer

An asthma attack can be brought on by various factors including allergy to pollen or dust (or fur), emotion, smoke and air pollution, exercise and even breathing in cold air. Treatment involves:

- removal of the factor causing the asthma attack
- use of an inhaler – usually a spray that relaxes the bronchial muscles.

Sufferers from asthma are advised not to smoke because this increases the chance of an attack. However, there are many other reasons why smoking is dangerous.

■ An asthma inhaler

Smoking and disease

In recent years there have been many health authority advertising campaigns that stress the harmful effects of smoking. At the same time the manufacturers of cigarettes try to reduce the impact of these campaigns by emphasising a glamorous side to smoking. But however the manufacturers try to reduce the impact of negative advertising, they still have to include, by law, a statement on adverts and on packaging that states that 'smoking can seriously damage your health'.

Companies involved in sales of life insurance policies now routinely ask people whether they smoke because they are aware of the effects of smoking on health.

How is smoking harmful?

Smoking involves inhaling smoke from burning tobacco and paper. This smoke can harm the lungs and respiratory passages for a number of reasons:

- it is hot
- it is dry
- it contains many harmful chemicals.

The simple experiment that follows can help to demonstrate the nasty chemicals in burning tobacco.

The dangers of tobacco smoke

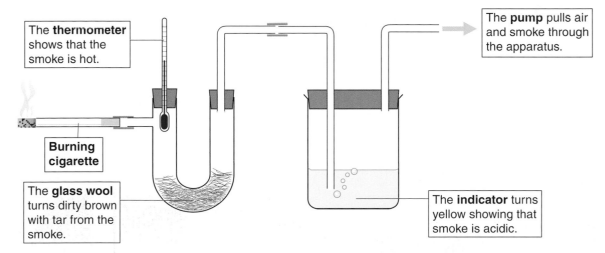

The **thermometer** shows that the smoke is hot.

The **pump** pulls air and smoke through the apparatus.

Burning cigarette

The **glass wool** turns dirty brown with tar from the smoke.

The **indicator** turns yellow showing that smoke is acidic.

Note: Universal Indicator changes colour from green to red/orange to show acidity. Hydrogen carbonate indicator changes colour from orange-red to yellow. The colour change you see in this experiment will depend on the indicator you use.

The heat and dryness caused by smoking irritate the lungs, but the main dangers of smoking relate to the chemicals in the burning tobacco. There are over 1000 known chemicals present in tobacco smoke. The most dangerous are tar, carbon monoxide and **nicotine** but there are even small quantities of arsenic and plutonium.

When doctors have to treat lung disease with medicine, the molecules of the medicine are always delivered in a spray form. Doctors know that the droplets of water can carry the helpful medicines right down through all of the respiratory tubes and deep into the lungs where they can carry out their useful work. Burning tobacco produces tiny droplets of water too, and these carry the harmful chemicals deep into the lungs in just the same way as medicines are delivered. It would be hard to find a more efficient way of delivering harmful chemicals to the lungs than smoking. Some of these dangerous chemicals, and the effects that they have on the body, are shown in the following diagram.

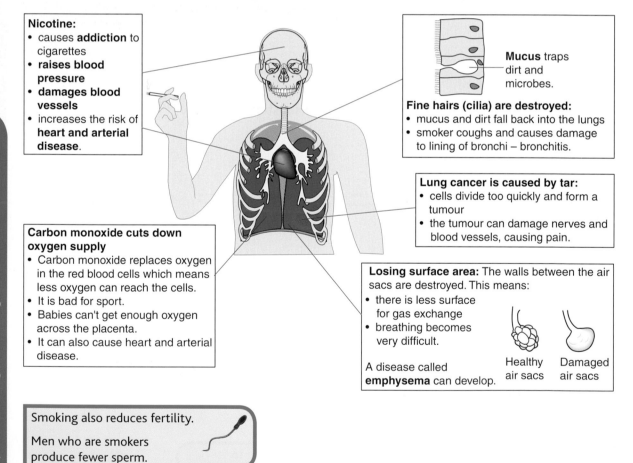

Nicotine:
- causes **addiction** to cigarettes
- **raises blood pressure**
- **damages blood vessels**
- increases the risk of **heart and arterial disease**.

Mucus traps dirt and microbes.

Fine hairs (cilia) are destroyed:
- mucus and dirt fall back into the lungs
- smoker coughs and causes damage to lining of bronchi – bronchitis.

Lung cancer is caused by tar:
- cells divide too quickly and form a tumour
- the tumour can damage nerves and blood vessels, causing pain.

Carbon monoxide cuts down oxygen supply
- Carbon monoxide replaces oxygen in the red blood cells which means less oxygen can reach the cells.
- It is bad for sport.
- Babies can't get enough oxygen across the placenta.
- It can also cause heart and arterial disease.

Losing surface area: The walls between the air sacs are destroyed. This means:
- there is less surface for gas exchange
- breathing becomes very difficult.

A disease called **emphysema** can develop.

Healthy air sacs

Damaged air sacs

Smoking also reduces fertility.

Men who are smokers produce fewer sperm.

◯ Preliminary knowledge: Smoking and the circulatory system

The circulatory system, which is shown right, is made up of three parts:

- the blood, a red fluid that can dissolve oxygen and foods
- the heart, that acts like a pump to push the blood around the body
- the blood vessels, the arteries, capillaries and veins, that make sure that the blood circulates to the places it's needed.

Arteries carry blood away from the heart and to the cells of the body.

Oxygen from lungs

Heart is the pump for the circulation.

Veins carry blood away from the cells and back to the heart.

Food from intestines

Capillaries allow food and gases to pass between the blood and the cells.

The heart pumps blood around the body by putting pressure on the blood and squeezing it into the blood vessels. The heart can do this because it is really one big mass of very powerful muscle. The structure of the heart is shown in the diagram below.

Artery going to the lungs carries blood with not much oxygen (and too much carbon dioxide).

Artery going to cells of the body carries blood with not a lot of food and oxygen.

Vein coming from body cells carries blood with not much oxygen but plenty of food.

Vein coming from lungs carries blood with a lot of oxygen.

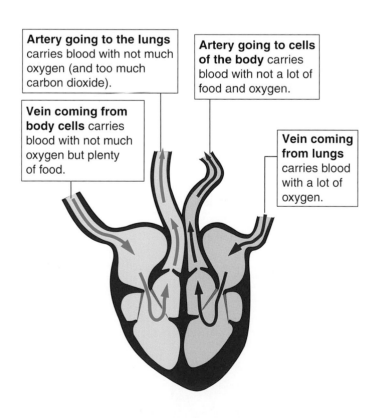

> **Did you know?**
> This muscle has a special feature - it never gets tired!

> **Did you know?**
> Even if you stand on your head your heart will continue to pump blood in the right direction around your body!

You can see that the heart is made up of four chambers. Two of the chambers receive blood, and two of them pump it out again.

Your heart beats often enough to keep delivering a good supply of food and oxygen to the cells that need these substances, even when you are asleep. Every beat of the heart makes the walls of the arteries stretch slightly. This 'stretching' can be felt anywhere that an artery passes over a bone near to the skin. This stretching movement is called a **pulse**. See the Chapter 6 section, 'Measuring exercise' for more information about your pulse and how to measure it.

Cigarettes also affect the heart and circulation

Smoking raises the pulse rate and the pressure in the blood vessels. Chemicals in the smoke also make it more likely that fatty substances will cause blockages in narrow blood vessels, including those in the brain and in the heart itself.

Nicotine in tobacco smoke is very quickly absorbed into the bloodstream. It is thought of as the most dangerous chemical present in tobacco smoke. The nicotine reaches the brain and gives smokers the pleasurable feeling that they crave, they become **addicted**. The nicotine also closes down some blood vessels, including the important arteries that supply the heart muscle with oxygen and glucose.

Smokers are therefore much more likely to have a heart attack or stroke than non-smokers.

Burning tobacco and paper give off a gas called **carbon monoxide**. This gas locks onto the oxygen-carrying chemical in your red blood cells. This means that your blood cannot carry as much oxygen as it should and you will lack energy, as well as seriously straining your heart. Pregnant women who smoke make it more difficult for their developing babies to get oxygen across the placenta. The babies grow more slowly and are lower in weight when they are born.

So don't forget!

- Smoking tobacco is harmful to the lungs and the circulation.
- There are many harmful components of tobacco smoke, but it is nicotine that causes addiction.
- It is very difficult to give up smoking, so it is better not to start in the first place!

Exercise 3.3: Smoking

1 This diagram shows a ciliated cell from the lining of the airway.

   (a) What is the function of this cell in the airway?

   (b) This cell is affected by substances in cigarette smoke. Suggest what effect cigarette smoke has on the cilia?

   (c) Give the name of the substance in cigarette smoke that causes addiction to smoking.

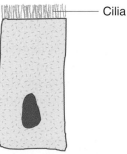

Cilia

2 The following graph shows the number of deaths from lung cancer in England and Wales between 1920 and 1960.

Working Scientifically

   (a) Between which two dates on the graph did the number of deaths from lung cancer rise fastest?

   (b) Describe the pattern shown by the data.

   (c) Suggest what this data might tell us about smoking rates during this period.

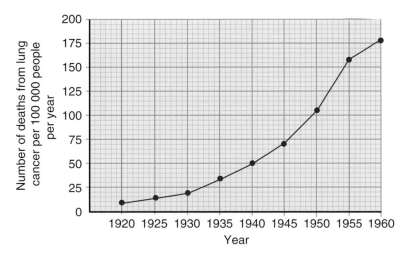

3 Lung cancer may be caused by smoking cigarettes.

   (a) Which substance in cigarette smoke causes lung cancer?

   (b) What effect does smoking have on the chances of developing heart disease?

Extension question

4 This table shows the causes of death of cigarette smokers in Great Britain.

Cause of death	Percentage of deaths
Lung cancer	8
Bronchitis and emphysema	17
Circulatory diseases	20
Other causes (not related to smoking)	55

(a) What percentage of smokers die from smoking-related diseases?

(b) Present the data in the form of a bar chart or a pie chart. Decide which is the best way to display the results. Explain your choice.

(c) Emphysema is a disease caused by smoking. The photo on the left shows normal lung tissue and the photo on the right shows lung tissue from a person with emphysema.

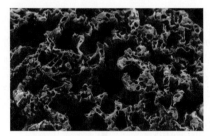 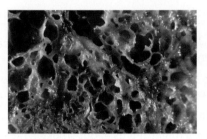

■ Air sacs (alveoli) in human lung tissue

■ A section of lung affected by emphysema

(i) Apart from colour, what differences do you notice between the normal lung tissue and lung tissue from a person with emphysema.

(ii) How will this difference affect the supply of oxygen to the blood in the person with emphysema?

(iii) Name two other diseases caused by smoking, and say what the symptoms would be (i.e. how the patient would be affected).

4 Reproduction in humans

Preliminary knowledge: The human life cycle

No organism lives forever. In order that species do not die out, individual organisms must be replaced.

Humans are no different. The human life cycle has several stages: from a developing fetus growing inside its mother, to a newborn baby, through childhood, adolescence, adulthood to old age. The life cycle ends with death.

Sexual reproduction in humans

Living organisms use the process of **reproduction** to produce new members of their species. Like all other mammals, humans only use **sexual reproduction**. Sexual reproduction involves the contribution of genetic information from two parents to produce a new individual.

Sexual reproduction involves a number of stages, and unless each of the stages is completed, sexual reproduction will be unsuccessful. The stages are:

1 The development of the body so that it can produce specialised sex cells called **gametes** (**sperm** in the male; **ova** (singular **ovum**) or eggs in the female).
2 The development of sex organs so that the gametes can be delivered by the male and received by the female.
3 The joining together of the gametes at **fertilisation** to produce a fertilised ovum (egg) called a **zygote**.
4 The development of a place for the safe growth of the zygote into an **embryo**, a **fetus** and, eventually, a baby.

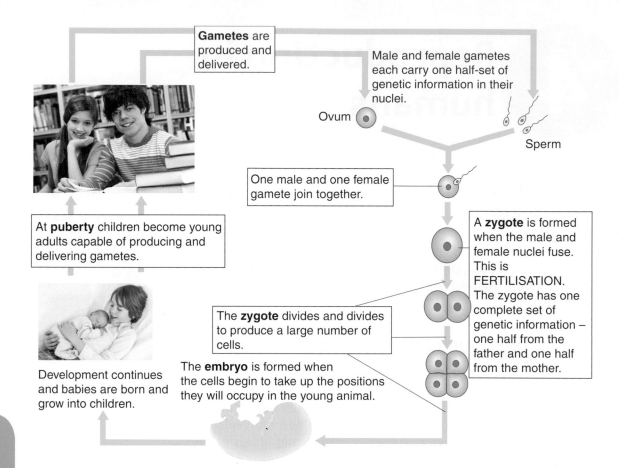

Gametes are produced and delivered.

Male and female gametes each carry one half-set of genetic information in their nuclei.

Ovum

Sperm

One male and one female gamete join together.

At **puberty** children become young adults capable of producing and delivering gametes.

A **zygote** is formed when the male and female nuclei fuse. This is FERTILISATION. The zygote has one complete set of genetic information – one half from the father and one half from the mother.

The **zygote** divides and divides to produce a large number of cells.

The **embryo** is formed when the cells begin to take up the positions they will occupy in the young animal.

Development continues and babies are born and grow into children.

The human reproductive systems

Adolescence is a time of change

When a young human grows, he or she passes through a period of physical and emotional development called **adolescence**. Adolescence can occur at any time between the ages of 10 and 20; every person is different and develops at different rates.

During adolescence a young person experiences a series of physical changes. We call this stage of development **puberty**. At puberty, the body develops a reproductive system that can complete the stages of sexual reproduction. The changes at puberty are controlled by chemicals from the brain and sex organs. These chemicals are the **sex hormones**.

The signs that puberty has taken place are shown in the following diagram.

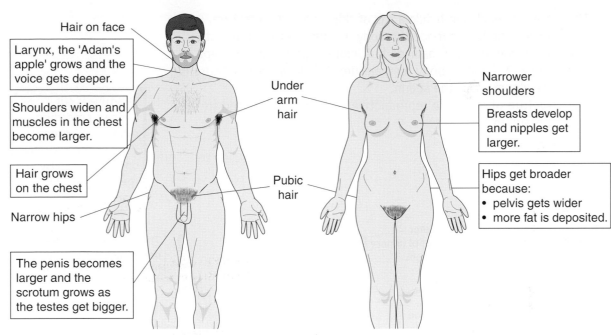

Hair on face

Larynx, the 'Adam's apple' grows and the voice gets deeper.

Shoulders widen and muscles in the chest become larger.

Hair grows on the chest

Narrow hips

The penis becomes larger and the scrotum grows as the testes get bigger.

Under arm hair

Pubic hair

Narrower shoulders

Breasts develop and nipples get larger.

Hips get broader because:
• pelvis gets wider
• more fat is deposited.

■ The physical changes of puberty

As well as physical changes, there are some **emotional and behavioural changes** that occur during adolesence.
During adolescence you may experience:

- mood swings
- aggression (boys)
- maternal instincts (girls).

During this period young people also:

- become more independent of their parents
- develop strong feelings of sexual attraction
- take on more responsibility for their behaviour.

This can be an exciting but confusing time. If you have any worries or questions find an adult you can talk to – a parent, relative or teacher.

The male reproductive system

The male reproductive system is simpler than the female reproductive system. It really has only two functions: firstly, to make the male gametes and secondly, to deliver them to the site of fertilisation.

The male gametes, called spermatozoa or **sperm** for short, are made in the **testes** (or testicles).

Go further

As well as making the sperm, the testes also produce the male sex hormone **testosterone**. This hormone is necessary for the action of the male sex organs and for controlling male sexual behaviour.

The testes are enclosed inside a sac of skin called the **scrotum**, which hangs between the legs outside the body. In this position the testes are protected from physical damage but, more importantly, are kept at a temperature 2–3 °C below body temperature. This lower temperature is ideal for development of the sperm.

The structure of the male reproductive system is illustrated in the following diagram.

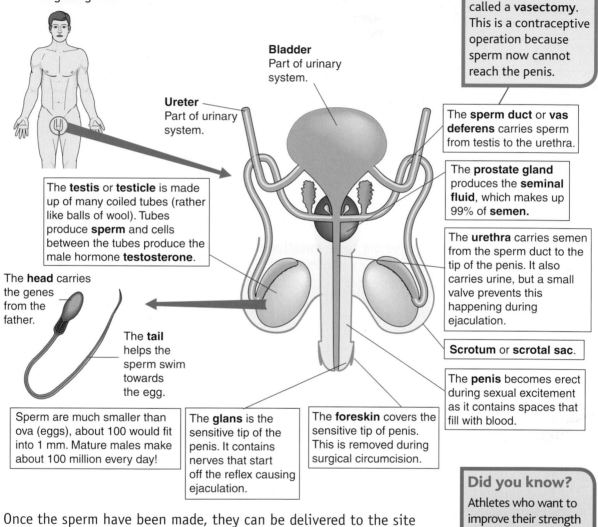

Bladder
Part of urinary system.

Ureter
Part of urinary system.

This tube is cut during a procedure called a **vasectomy**. This is a contraceptive operation because sperm now cannot reach the penis.

The **sperm duct** or **vas deferens** carries sperm from testis to the urethra.

The **prostate gland** produces the **seminal fluid**, which makes up 99% of **semen.**

The **testis** or **testicle** is made up of many coiled tubes (rather like balls of wool). Tubes produce **sperm** and cells between the tubes produce the male hormone **testosterone**.

The **urethra** carries semen from the sperm duct to the tip of the penis. It also carries urine, but a small valve prevents this happening during ejaculation.

The **head** carries the genes from the father.

The **tail** helps the sperm swim towards the egg.

Scrotum or **scrotal sac**.

The **penis** becomes erect during sexual excitement as it contains spaces that fill with blood.

Sperm are much smaller than ova (eggs), about 100 would fit into 1 mm. Mature males make about 100 million every day!

The **glans** is the sensitive tip of the penis. It contains nerves that start off the reflex causing ejaculation.

The **foreskin** covers the sensitive tip of penis. This is removed during surgical circumcision.

Once the sperm have been made, they can be delivered to the site of fertilisation through the **penis**. The release of sperm is called ejaculation. To help their release and increase the chances of fertilisation, the sperm are released in a fluid, the **semen.**

To perform its function of sperm delivery the human penis only needs to be 9–10 cm long when fully erect.

Many mammals, but not humans, have a bone, called the *os penis* or baculum, to hold the penis erect. The penis slides back into the body following intercourse.

Did you know?
Athletes who want to improve their strength and power sometimes take hormones that are very similar to testosterone. This behaviour is not allowed and if the athletes are caught, they are usually banned from competing.

The female reproductive system

The reproductive system of the female is more complicated than that of the male. As well as producing female gametes, the female system must also receive male gametes (sperm) and provide a site for fertilisation and for the development of the zygote (see 'Fertilisation and conception', later in this chapter).

The gametes, called **ova** (or eggs), are produced in the two **ovaries**. An ovum travels towards the **uterus** (womb) in the **oviducts** (fallopian tubes). This is where fertilisation occurs and it is in the uterus that the development of the zygote into a new baby takes place. The **vagina** has a dual function. Firstly, it receives the penis, and secondly it acts as a birth canal for the eventual delivery of the baby from its mother's body. The female reproductive system is illustrated in the following diagram.

> **Did you know?**
>
> The vagina is a hostile environment for sperm! Bacteria that live on the wall of the vagina produce acids, as do some of the female's own cells. These acids harm sperm and stop them swimming, so seminal fluids include an alkali to neutralise the secretions of the vagina and allow some sperm to survive. You will learn about acids, alkalis and neutralisation in Chemistry, Chapter 9.

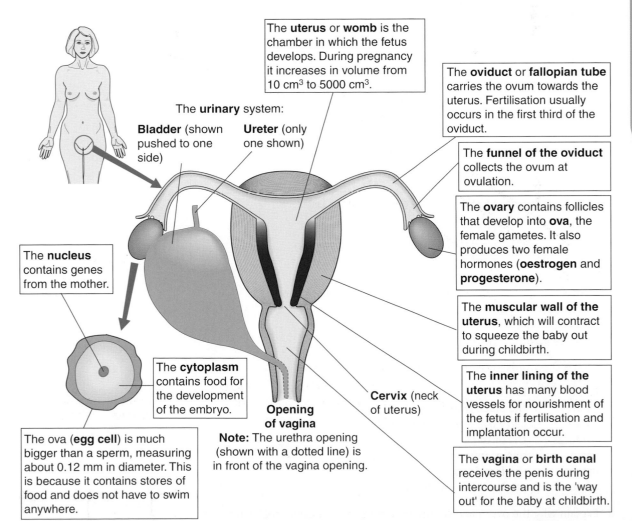

The **uterus** or **womb** is the chamber in which the fetus develops. During pregnancy it increases in volume from 10 cm³ to 5000 cm³.

The **urinary** system:

Bladder (shown pushed to one side)

Ureter (only one shown)

The **nucleus** contains genes from the mother.

The **cytoplasm** contains food for the development of the embryo.

Opening of vagina

Note: The urethra opening (shown with a dotted line) is in front of the vagina opening.

The ova (**egg cell**) is much bigger than a sperm, measuring about 0.12 mm in diameter. This is because it contains stores of food and does not have to swim anywhere.

The **oviduct** or **fallopian tube** carries the ovum towards the uterus. Fertilisation usually occurs in the first third of the oviduct.

The **funnel of the oviduct** collects the ovum at ovulation.

The **ovary** contains follicles that develop into **ova**, the female gametes. It also produces two female hormones (**oestrogen** and **progesterone**).

The **muscular wall of the uterus**, which will contract to squeeze the baby out during childbirth.

Cervix (neck of uterus)

The **inner lining of the uterus** has many blood vessels for nourishment of the fetus if fertilisation and implantation occur.

The **vagina** or **birth canal** receives the penis during intercourse and is the 'way out' for the baby at childbirth.

51

1 Look at this diagram and identify each of the structures A–G.

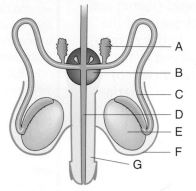

2 Look at this diagram and identify each of the structures A–F.

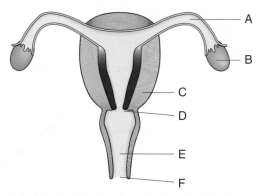

3 Match the words in List 1 with the descriptions in List 2.

List 1:   **List 2:**
testes   produces a fluid for sperm to swim in
sperm   carries sperm from testes to the penis
semen   delivers sperm in semen to the vagina
scrotum   produce the sperm and the male sex hormone
sperm duct   hold the testes outside the body
penis   a fluid for the sperm to swim in
prostate gland   the male gamete

4 Match the words in List A with the descriptions in List B.

List A: **List B:**
ovaries   the place where the baby develops
ovum   carry ova from ovaries to uterus
oviducts   the birth canal
vagina   ring of muscle at neck of uterus
uterus   the female gamete
cervix   produce the female gametes

5 Explain why the ovum and sperm are different from each other. Give one important way in which they are the same as each other.

The menstrual cycle

As you have learned, boys and girls go through a stage of development in adolescence called puberty. Puberty prepares the body for sexual reproduction. Following puberty, girls begin to release mature ova (eggs) from their ovaries.

Both the testes in males and the ovaries in females produce the sex cells or gametes (sperm in males and ova in females). However, they differ in how often they work and in the number of gametes they produce. Males continue to produce sperm at the rate of about 100 000 000 (one hundred million) per day from puberty to old age. Females, however, are born with all the ova (or eggs) that they will ever have. The ova mature and are released from the ovaries at the rate of only one per month from puberty until the time known as **menopause** (which usually occurs between the ages of 45–55). In fact, each ovary takes about two months (around 56 days) to produce a mature ovum. The two ovaries are a month out of phase with one another so that the female reproductive system actually releases one ovum around every 28 days.

The cycle of producing and releasing mature ova is called the **menstrual cycle** (from the Latin word *menstruus*, meaning 'monthly'). The cycle is summarised in the following diagram.

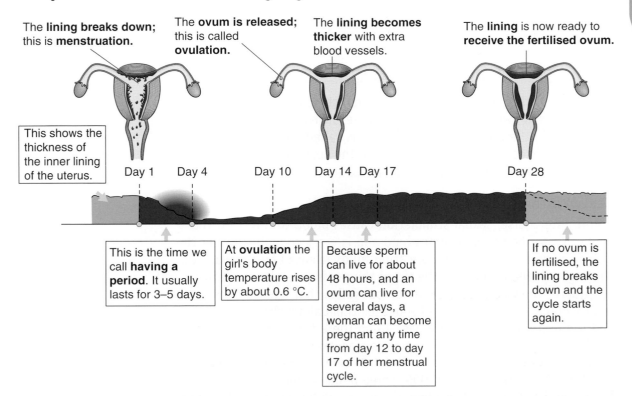

The **lining breaks down**; this is **menstruation**.

The **ovum is released**; this is called **ovulation**.

The **lining becomes thicker** with extra blood vessels.

The **lining** is now ready to **receive the fertilised ovum**.

This shows the thickness of the inner lining of the uterus.

Day 1   Day 4   Day 10   Day 14 Day 17   Day 28

This is the time we call **having a period**. It usually lasts for 3–5 days.

At **ovulation** the girl's body temperature rises by about 0.6 °C.

Because sperm can live for about 48 hours, and an ovum can live for several days, a woman can become pregnant any time from day 12 to day 17 of her menstrual cycle.

If no ovum is fertilised, the lining breaks down and the cycle starts again.

The menstrual cycle has two important roles:

- **To prepare the uterus to receive any fertilised ova**: During the menstrual cycle the wall of the uterus goes through several stages that prepare the inner lining of the uterus to receive a fertilised ovum. This involves growing extra blood vessels in the wall of the uterus. If no fertilised ovum is present, this inner lining breaks down and is passed out through the vagina. This is called menstruation. Menstruation marks the end of one menstrual cycle and the start of the next one. The girl will notice a loss of blood when this happens; this is known as 'having a period'.
- **To control the development and release of mature ova**: During the menstrual cycle only properly developed ova are released from the ovaries at the correct time. An ovum is released halfway through the menstrual cycle in a process called ovulation.

Following ovulation, the ovum moves slowly along the oviduct towards the uterus. This movement is helped by:

- contractions of muscles in the wall of the oviduct that squeeze the ovum towards the uterus
- fine hairs on the lining of the oviduct that sweep the ovum in the right direction.

It takes about 4–7 days for the ovum to reach the uterus. During this time, fertilisation of the ovum may take place.

Fertilisation and conception

If a sperm finds a mature ovum in the oviduct, it will fuse with it in a process known as fertilisation. The resulting zygote becomes implanted in the wall of the uterus. This is called conception.

Before this can happen, the ovum and the sperm must meet and this is the purpose of copulation or sexual intercourse.

Sexual intercourse delivers male gametes

Before intercourse, sexual stimulation causes blood to flow into the man's penis. The penis becomes hard and is erect enough to enter the woman's vagina (helped by lubricating fluids released by the walls of the vagina). The rubbing of the tip of the penis (the glans) against the wall of the vagina sets off a nervous reflex that releases sperm from storage in the testes, and squeezes them along the sperm ducts and the urethra. As the sperm pass along these tubes, fluid is added to them so that the complete semen is ejaculated in spurts from the tip of the penis. There is usually about 3–4 cm^3 of semen ejaculated, which contains up to 300 000 000 (three hundred million) sperm. The following diagrams illustrate how the male and female gametes arrive at the same place.

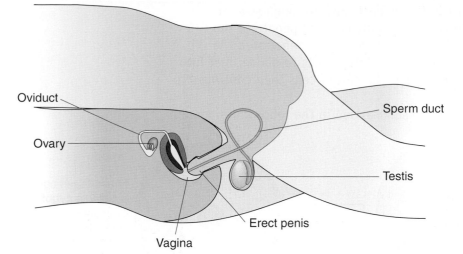

■ Sexual intercourse delivers the male gametes (sperm) to the female reproductive system

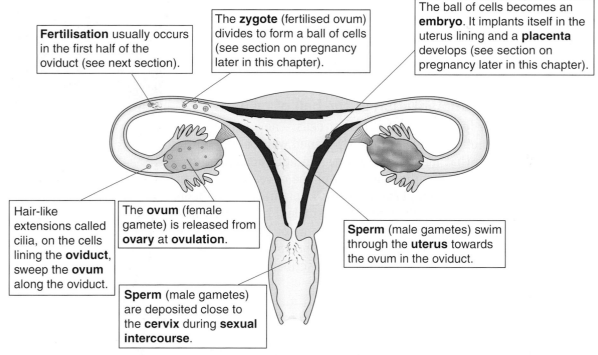

Fertilisation usually occurs in the first half of the oviduct (see next section).

The **zygote** (fertilised ovum) divides to form a ball of cells (see section on pregnancy later in this chapter).

The ball of cells becomes an **embryo**. It implants itself in the uterus lining and a **placenta** develops (see section on pregnancy later in this chapter).

Hair-like extensions called cilia, on the cells lining the **oviduct**, sweep the **ovum** along the oviduct.

The **ovum** (female gamete) is released from **ovary** at **ovulation**.

Sperm (male gametes) swim through the **uterus** towards the ovum in the oviduct.

Sperm (male gametes) are deposited close to the **cervix** during **sexual intercourse**.

■ Following intercourse the sperm swim to the site of fertilisation of the ovum (female gamete) in the oviduct

Fertilisation involves the fusion of ovum and sperm

As you have learned, fertilisation is the joining together, or **fusion**, of an ovum and a sperm. The head of a sperm enters the ovum, leaving its tail behind. This process allows a set of genes from the mother and a set of genes from the father to be mixed together when the nuclei of both cells fuse together. As a result, the new individual will have some characteristics from each of the parents.

Fertilisation takes place in the oviduct, and although several hundred sperm may reach the ovum, only one will penetrate the membrane that surrounds it. Once the sperm has penetrated the membrane, the fertilised ovum (the zygote) starts to divide, first into two cells, then into four and so on. The ball of cells then continues to move towards the uterus.

The events of fertilisation are summarised in the following diagram.

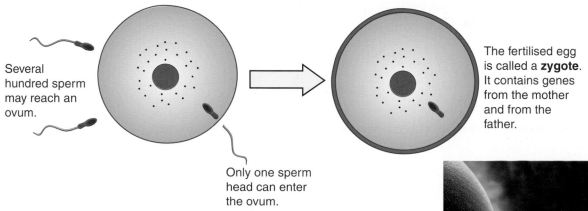

Several hundred sperm may reach an ovum.

Only one sperm head can enter the ovum.

The fertilised egg is called a **zygote**. It contains genes from the mother and from the father.

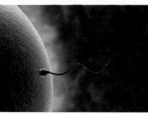

■ A sperm fusing with an ovum at the moment of fertilisation. On the right is an image showing the relative sizes of both gametes.

Conception is the implantation of the ball of cells

About six days after fertilisation, the ball of cells – now called an **embryo** – becomes embedded in the thickened wall of the uterus. It is possible that many fertilised ova do not complete this process. In fact, conception, the beginning of the development of a new individual, has not taken place until this implantation has been completed successfully. Once the embryo is attached to the wall of the uterus, some of its outer cells combine with some of the mother's cells and a **placenta** begins to develop. The importance of the placenta in the development of the new individual is described later in this chapter.

Exercise 4.2: Menstruation and fertilisation

1 Match up the processes named in List A with the descriptions in List B.

List A	List B
Ovulation	Sexual intercourse
Ejaculation	Ovum and sperm joining together
Menstruation	The release of a mature female gamete
Fertilisation	When a fertilised ovum sticks to the wall of the uterus
Conception	The release of sperm in the semen
Copulation	The breakdown and release of the inner lining of the uterus

Pregnancy

As you have learned, an ovum (egg) fertilised by a sperm forms a zygote. A zygote contains genes from both mother and father. The zygote becomes attached to the wall of the uterus at conception. The production of the new baby involves two linked processes.

- **Growth**: The original zygote has to divide to provide the many cells that make up the baby.
- **Development**: The organisation of the many cells into different tissues and organs.

The growth stages involve the division of the zygote into many identical copies. One zygote at conception becomes thirty million million cells at birth. As the cells are produced, each one takes up its correct position in the embryo. As they become organised into particular tissues they begin to take on special functions (see the section on specialisation in Chapter 1). For example, quite early on during pregnancy it is possible to recognise nerve cells and skin cells.

These first steps in the development of a human baby, from the growth and development of a zygote, are outlined in the following diagram.

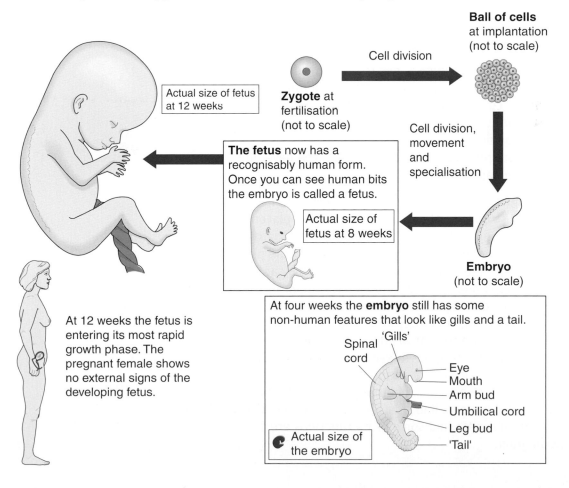

Actual size of fetus at 12 weeks

Zygote at fertilisation (not to scale)

Cell division

Ball of cells at implantation (not to scale)

Cell division, movement and specialisation

The fetus now has a recognisably human form. Once you can see human bits the embryo is called a fetus.

Actual size of fetus at 8 weeks

Embryo (not to scale)

At 12 weeks the fetus is entering its most rapid growth phase. The pregnant female shows no external signs of the developing fetus.

At four weeks the **embryo** still has some non-human features that look like gills and a tail.

Spinal cord

'Gills'

Eye
Mouth
Arm bud
Umbilical cord
Leg bud
'Tail'

Actual size of the embryo

> **Did you know?**
>
> Even before the female's abdomen begins to swell, there are changes that can show that she's pregnant:
>
> - There is no monthly period.
> - Hormones from the placenta spill over into her urine. These are detected using a pregnancy test kit.
>
> At about 5 months old, the fetus begins to kick and punch and the mother-to-be can feel this movement.

The role of the placenta

The time taken for the development of a baby from an implanted zygote is called the gestation period. We say that the mother is **pregnant** during this period. In humans this is normally around 9 months or 40 weeks. During this time the mother provides a stable environment for the developing fetus. The mother controls the important factors of the fetus' environment:

- the supply of soluble nutrients, such as glucose and minerals, for the growth of new cells
- the removal of waste materials, such as carbon dioxide, which could be poisonous to the fetus
- the supply of oxygen, which is necessary for the release of energy in aerobic respiration (cell division requires a great deal of energy)
- maintaining a constant body temperature
- protection from the risk of infection by micro-organisms in the outside environment
- protection from physical shock or damage – the developing nervous system is especially fragile.

The supply of nutrients and oxygen and the removal of waste are carried out by a structure called the placenta. The placenta is formed partly from the lining of the uterus and partly from the outside cells of the developing embryo. The fetus is attached to the placenta by the **umbilical cord** and is surrounded by a sac. This sac is called the **amniotic sac** and is filled with a fluid called the amniotic fluid. The placenta begins to develop as soon as the embryo becomes implanted in the wall of the uterus and after about 12 weeks it is a thick, saucer-shaped structure that grows deep into the wall of the uterus. The placenta continues to grow to keep pace with the developing fetus and at the time of birth it is about 15 cm across and weighs about 500 g. After the baby has been born, the placenta, amniotic sac and umbilical cord are expelled from the uterus as the **afterbirth**. The structure of the placenta and some of its functions are shown in the following diagram.

The **artery** carries carbon dioxide and other waste from the developing baby to the placenta.

The **umbilical cord** connects the embryo/fetus to the placenta.

Wall of uterus (womb)

An **embryo** needs food and oxygen and must get rid of carbon dioxide.

The **mother's blood** brings food and oxygen to the placenta.

The **mother's blood** carries waste away from the placenta.

The **amniotic sac** contains a fluid that acts like a cushion against bumps as the mother gets on with her daily life.

A **vein** carries food and oxygen from the placenta back to the developing baby.

The **placenta** has thin walls and lots of folds that make it easy to exchange food and oxygen for waste.

Some harmful substances can cross from the mother to her developing baby:

- alcohol – which may cause brain damage to the baby
- gaseous chemicals from smoking – which may reduce the baby's birth weight
- nicotine from smoking – a baby can be a nicotine addict when it is born
- viruses – babies can be born with HIV or other sexually transmitted viruses if the mother is infected.

Pregnant women are therefore advised not to drink alcohol or smoke during pregnancy.

Did you know?

Doctors can take a sample of the amniotic fluid during pregnancy and do tests on it to find out:

- whether the baby is a boy or a girl
- whether the baby might need special medical treatment once it has been born.

The removal of a sample of amniotic fluid carries a small risk of the baby being lost (miscarriage).

Exchange of materials across the placenta

The placenta is the point of contact between the blood systems of the fetus and the mother. It has a number of adaptations that make sure the correct materials cross quickly enough to keep a safe and stable environment for the fetus.

- It has a large surface area, which allows more molecules to cross the placenta in any unit of time.
- The blood of the mother is always separated from the blood of the fetus by membranes that control which molecules cross from mother to fetus. The blood of the mother and her developing baby never mix.
- The fetus has arteries inside the umbilical cord that deliver blood to the placenta and a vein that returns from the placenta, carrying absorbed substances.

Birth

By the end of pregnancy the baby normally lies in the uterus with its head close to the cervix. A doctor or midwife can tell that birth is near when the baby has moved into this position. The birth can be separated into a number of stages. Together these stages are called **labour**. Labour may last from one hour to twelve hours (or even longer).

Labour begins with the first **contractions** of the muscle of the uterus. These contractions are controlled by hormones. Some of these chemical messages come from the mother and some come from the baby.

At first the contractions come every 20 minutes or so, but as birth approaches they happen more often and with more power. The contractions break the **amniotic membrane** and release the amniotic fluid – this is known as the **breaking of the waters** – and make the cervix dilate (get wider). The first stage of labour is complete when the cervix is wide enough for the baby's head to pass through.

Labour continues as the baby's head is pushed past the cervix into the vagina, which now acts as a birth canal. From now on the process is quite rapid and needs only gentle contractions by the mother, helped by the midwife or the obstetrician (a doctor who specialises in births).

The birth process can be quite stressful for the baby. It may become short of oxygen as the umbilical cord is squeezed by the walls of the birth canal. The baby's heartbeat is carefully checked during birth and the blood soon re-oxygenates when the baby begins to take a few breaths. Once the doctor is satisfied that the baby is breathing properly, the umbilical cord is clamped to prevent bleeding and cut. The mother and child are now two separate individuals.

Exercise 4.3: Placenta and birth

1 Copy and complete the following paragraphs about the birth of a human baby. Use words from this list:

uterus	amniotic sac	umbilical	oxygen
afterbirth	vagina	cervix	placenta

(a) An expectant mother knows when she is about to give birth because her _____ begins to experience waves of contractions. Eventually the contractions are so powerful that the _____ dilates, the _____ bursts and the waters are released.

(b) Further powerful contractions push the baby through the _____ or birth canal. Once the baby has been delivered, it is important that it takes deep breaths because it may have been deprived of _____ as the _____ cord is compressed during delivery. This cord is clamped and cut, and gentle contractions of the uterus cause the _____ to come away from the wall of the uterus and pass out of the vagina as the _____.

2 Look at these two diagrams. Use words from this list to identify the structures that are labelled A–H on the diagrams. Words may be used more than once.

embryo	fetus	placenta
amniotic fluid	umbilical cord	cervix
amniotic sac	wall of uterus	

(a)

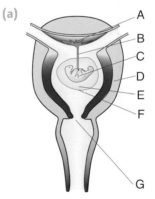

■ An embryo in the uterus at about 4 weeks old

(b)

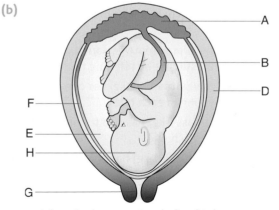

■ A fetus in the uterus just before birth

Extension question

3 The following table provides information about a range of mammals, including the gestation period (time between fertilisation and birth).

Species	Mass of adult/ kilograms	Gestation period/days	Number of litters per year	Number of young per litter
Cat	4	60	2	3 to 5
Chimpanzee	75	270	1	1
Elephant	7000	640	$\frac{1}{2}$ (1 per 2 years)	1
Horse	1300	335	1	1
Mouse	0.025	21	5	4 to 8
Pig	300	115	2	6 to 16
Rabbit	1.5	30	3	4 to 10
Rat	0.5	22	2 to 6	5 to 15

(a) A scatter diagram is a type of graph used to show whether there is any correlation between two groups of information. Use a scatter diagram to see whether there is any correlation between the mass of an adult animal and its gestation period. Plot mass on the *x*-axis and gestation period on the *y*-axis.

(b) Estimate the approximate gestation period of the following mammals. Justify your estimate by referring to the data in the table.

    (i) A hedgehog (mass 0.8 kg) has one or two litters per year with three to six young in each one.

    (ii) A hare (mass 5 kg) has two to three litters per year with two to five young in each one.

    (iii) A tiger (mass 300 kg) has one litter per year with two to four young in it.

The life of the plant: reproduction

Like any other organism, an individual plant will eventually die. For a particular *species* of plant to survive, the *individual* plants of that species must be able to reproduce themselves. This process of **reproduction** is needed as part of the life cycle of a plant. The life cycle of a flowering plant is shown in the following diagram. Look at the different stages and see how each stage leads on to the next one.

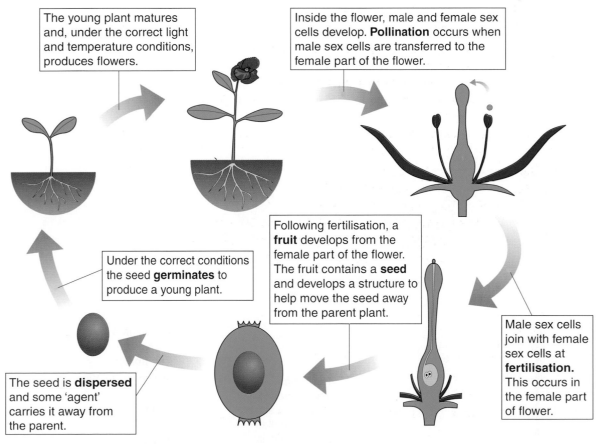

The young plant matures and, under the correct light and temperature conditions, produces flowers.

Inside the flower, male and female sex cells develop. **Pollination** occurs when male sex cells are transferred to the female part of the flower.

Under the correct conditions the seed **germinates** to produce a young plant.

Following fertilisation, a **fruit** develops from the female part of the flower. The fruit contains a **seed** and develops a structure to help move the seed away from the parent plant.

Male sex cells join with female sex cells at **fertilisation.** This occurs in the female part of flower.

The seed is **dispersed** and some 'agent' carries it away from the parent.

■ The life cycle of a flowering plant

⃝ Preliminary knowledge: The structure of flowers

As you saw in the previous diagram, the **flower** is the important organ in the reproduction of flowing plants. A flower grows from a bud, which is found at the end of a flower stalk. The flower is made up of **petals** that surround the special parts of the plant that make the sex cells. The petals are usually the most obvious part of the flower. They often have bright colours and a pleasant smell. It is these two features that help the flower attract insects. Insects can be very important in transferring the sex cells between different flowers. We will see why this is important in the next section.

There are two parts of the flower that actually make the sex cells. In the centre of the flower, the **carpel** can be found. This is the female part of the flower. The female sex cells called **ovules** are made in the **ovary** at the bottom of the carpel. The male parts of the flower are the **stamens** and they grow in a circle around the carpel. The male sex cells, known as the **pollen**, are made in the **anthers** at the top of the stamens.

The structure of an insect-pollinated flower is shown in the following diagram. There are many different types of flower. They are different from each other because the pollination stage in the life cycle of the plant can be carried out in different ways, which we will explore in the next section.

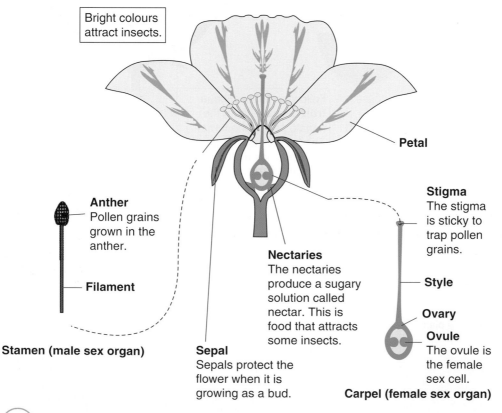

Bright colours attract insects.

Anther
Pollen grains grown in the anther.

Filament

Stamen (male sex organ)

Nectaries
The nectaries produce a sugary solution called nectar. This is food that attracts some insects.

Sepal
Sepals protect the flower when it is growing as a bud.

Petal

Stigma
The stigma is sticky to trap pollen grains.

Style

Ovary

Ovule
The ovule is the female sex cell.

Carpel (female sex organ)

Exercise 5.1: Flower structure

1 Match the parts of a flower in the left-hand column with the correct function from the right-hand column.

Flower parts	Functions
(a) pollen	1 supports the anther
(b) flower stalk	2 make a sweet, sugary solution
(c) style	3 contains the female sex cells
(d) filament	4 protects the flower in bud
(e) anther	5 delivers the male sex cells
(f) stigma	6 forms a base for the flower
(g) petal	7 holds up the stigma
(h) nectaries	8 attracts insects
(i) ovary	9 produces pollen
(j) sepal	10 receives pollen

2 Draw a simple diagram of an insect-pollinated flower, labelling all the flower parts from the list above.

Pollination and fertilisation

Remember:

- the transfer of male sex cells to female sex cells in plants is called **pollination**
- flowers are the reproductive part of a plant
- stamens produce the male sex cells, which are called **pollen grains**
- the carpel, containing the female sex cell (**ovum**), receives the male sex cells.

Agents of pollination

Individual plants cannot move very much at all. For sexual reproduction to occur, the male sex cells must be carried to the female part of the flower. This may be a very simple process, with the pollen just being transferred from the anther to the stigma of the same flower. However, it is better if the pollen grains can be carried to a different flower, so some 'helping hand' or 'agent' is needed to carry the pollen grains from the anthers of one flower to the stigma of another. This is most often an insect or the wind and so we say that plants are either insect-pollinated or wind-pollinated.

We have already seen the structure of a typical insect-pollinated flower. The following diagram shows how the structure of a wind-pollinated flower is adapted to successful pollination.

Tiny petal: helps to push the bracts apart to expose stigma and stamens.

Anthers: are held at the middle so that they can shake to release the pollen.

Stigma: long and feathery to give a large surface area for pollen to land on. Often hang out into the wind.

Filaments: long and flexible so that anthers are held out into the wind.

Pollen: light and produced in huge quantities. Has smooth coat and tiny 'wings' to help transfer by the wind.

Wind-pollinated flowers are often produced at colder times of the year when very few insects are flying.

They have no nectar or scent as they do not need to attract insects.

Pollination is complete once the pollen from an anther has landed on the stigma of the same or another flower. The next step in the plant's life cycle is fertilisation.

Fertilisation

Fertilisation occurs when the male and female sex cells join together. This process goes on deep in the ovary of the flower.

Here are some important points to learn about this part of the process.

- The male sex cell of a flower is inside the pollen grain and the female sex cell is inside the ovule.
- For fertilisation to take place the male sex cell in the pollen grain on the stigma must be able to reach the female sex cell, inside the ovule in the ovary.
- This is possible because a **pollen tube** grows out of the pollen grain when the grain lands on the surface of the stigma.
- The tube grows down through the style, through the ovary wall and eventually enters the ovule through a small hole.
- The male sex cell can then travel down the pollen tube, enter the ovule and join with the female sex cell.

This process is explained in the following diagram.

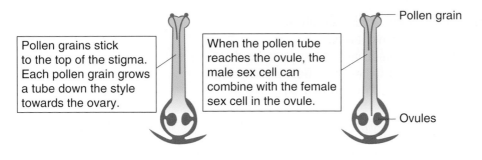

Pollen grains stick to the top of the stigma. Each pollen grain grows a tube down the style towards the ovary.

When the pollen tube reaches the ovule, the male sex cell can combine with the female sex cell in the ovule.

Pollen grain

Ovules

Fertilisation also starts the production of food stores inside the ovule. These food stores will be necessary for the development of the embryo and the early growth of the seedling before the young plant is able to photosynthesise for itself.

The formation of fruit and seed

After the male sex cell has joined with the female sex cell, the fertilised egg divides many times to produce an **embryo**. The embryo is made up of a tiny **shoot** and a tiny **root** together with two special leaves that can act as **food stores**. The outside of the ovule becomes hard to form a **seed coat**. Together the embryo and the seed coat make up a **seed**. The structure of a seed is shown in the following diagram.

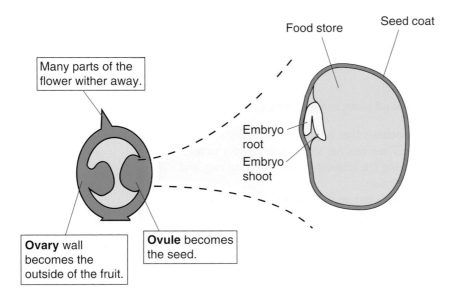

Food store

Seed coat

Many parts of the flower wither away.

Embryo root

Embryo shoot

Ovary wall becomes the outside of the fruit.

Ovule becomes the seed.

After fertilisation, the seed sends messages to the flower. These messages make the flower change.

- The sepals and petals wither away, and may fall off.
- The stamens, stigma and style wither away.
- The wall of the ovary changes: sometimes it becomes hard and dry, like a walnut; sometimes it becomes fleshy and juicy, like a plum; it can even become tough and leathery, like a sunflower seed.

The ovary is now called a **fruit**. The fruit has the function of dispersing the seeds away from the parent plant (see next section).

Exercise 5.2: Pollination and fertilisation

1 (a) What is the difference between pollination and fertilisation?
  (b) Explain the process of pollination.
  (c) Explain what happens during fertilisation and draw a simple diagram to illustrate the process.
2 How does the structure of a flower help in pollination?
3 Make a simple diagram of a typical flower. On your diagram label:
  (a) the parts that fall off after fertilisation
  (b) the parts that develop into a fruit.

Extension questions
4 Which of the following are
  (a) fruits
  (b) seeds
  (c) neither fruit nor seed?
    tomato, cucumber, sprout, baked bean, runner bean, celery, pea, grape

5 Two students came up with a hypothesis that a flower cannot produce fruits unless pollination has taken place. Their teacher showed them how to prevent bees reaching the flowers by covering the flowers in a fine netting bag, and how to transfer pollen with a paintbrush.
  Describe how the students could carry out an investigation to test their hypothesis. In your answer be sure to describe:

- any controls that they could include
- any steps they could take to ensure the results were valid.

Working Scientifically

Dispersal of seeds and fruits

Remember:

- A seed is formed after fertilisation.
- The seed is inside the part of the flower that has not withered away.
- The seed and the ovary together make up the fruit.

The seed contains an embryo plant. Before it can develop into a new young plant the seed must be separated from its parent plant. The new young plant, like its parent, will need water, carbon dioxide, minerals and light to grow. If the young plant is too close to the parent, it will struggle to get enough of these essential substances. The parent plant develops a way of scattering the seeds so that the young plants will be far enough away. This scattering is called **seed dispersal**. Fruits are adapted in many ways to help dispersal of the seeds, as the following diagram shows.

Animals and wind help with both pollination **and** seed dispersal. Do not get them mixed up.

Did you know?

Coconut 'milk' is actually the liquid part of the food for the seed when it germinates.

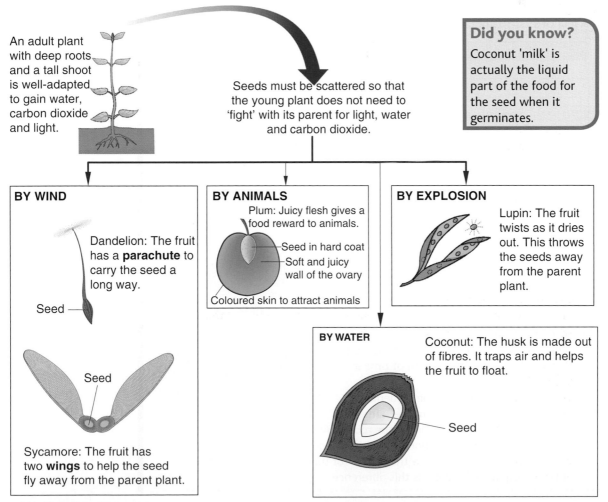

An adult plant with deep roots and a tall shoot is well-adapted to gain water, carbon dioxide and light.

Seeds must be scattered so that the young plant does not need to 'fight' with its parent for light, water and carbon dioxide.

BY WIND

Dandelion: The fruit has a **parachute** to carry the seed a long way.

Seed

Seed

Sycamore: The fruit has two **wings** to help the seed fly away from the parent plant.

BY ANIMALS

Plum: Juicy flesh gives a food reward to animals.

Seed in hard coat
Soft and juicy wall of the ovary

Coloured skin to attract animals

BY EXPLOSION

Lupin: The fruit twists as it dries out. This throws the seeds away from the parent plant.

BY WATER

Coconut: The husk is made out of fibres. It traps air and helps the fruit to float.

Seed

■ Dispersal of seeds

Investigation: Adaptation to wind dispersal

The individual parachutes from a dandelion fruit can be dropped to the ground.

Measure the time taken for a dropped dandelion fruit to reach the ground, and the distance travelled by the fruit in that time.

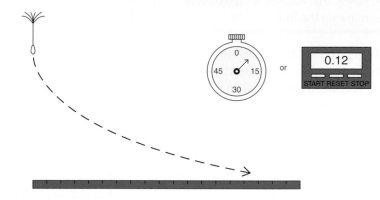

Repeat the procedure ten times and record the results in a suitable table.

A pair of students obtained the following results.

Time taken/seconds	Distance travelled/cm
3	65
9	140
11	170
6	100
14	200
7	105
9	135
7	95
2	45
8	165

1 Plot this information as a scatter graph.
2 Is there any relationship between the time spent floating and the efficiency of dispersal of the dandelion fruit?
3 Look at the image of dandelion fruits. Is there any part of the structure of the fruit that would increase the length of time it spent floating?

4 The teacher insisted that the students dropped all of the fruits from the same height and in the same corner of the room. Why?
5 The same kind of investigation can be carried out with sycamore fruits or with blueberries. Suggest how the results for these two fruits would be different. Explain why there is this difference.

Preliminary knowledge: Germination of seeds

Once the seeds are scattered, hopefully landing some distance away from the parent plant, the seed can begin to grow. Remember from the previous section, a seed is made up of a tiny new plant called an embryo plus a food store. If the seed can get enough **water**, **oxygen** and **warmth**, then the embryo begins to grow. This process is called **germination**. Germination does not require light; most seeds germinate underground.

During the process of germination, the food stores inside the seed are used to make leaves and roots. Once the young plant has its own leaves and roots, it can begin making its own food by photosynthesis.

Germination of most seeds follows the pattern shown in the following diagram.

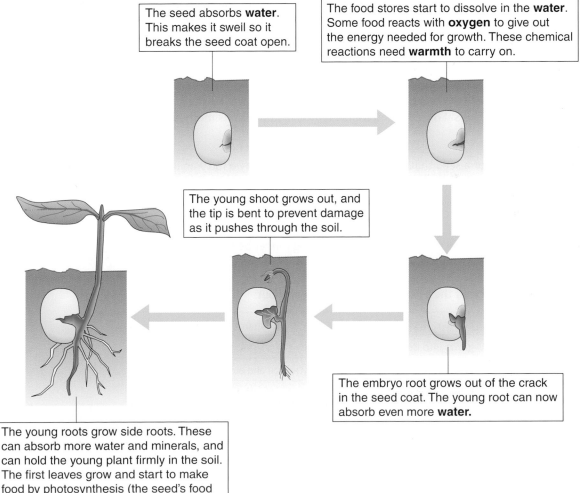

The seed absorbs **water**. This makes it swell so it breaks the seed coat open.

The food stores start to dissolve in the **water**. Some food reacts with **oxygen** to give out the energy needed for growth. These chemical reactions need **warmth** to carry on.

The young shoot grows out, and the tip is bent to prevent damage as it pushes through the soil.

The embryo root grows out of the crack in the seed coat. The young root can now absorb even more **water**.

The young roots grow side roots. These can absorb more water and minerals, and can hold the young plant firmly in the soil. The first leaves grow and start to make food by photosynthesis (the seed's food is now all used up).

Exercise 5.3: Dispersal and germination

1 Copy and complete the paragraph below about reproduction in plants. Use words from this list:

dispersal reproduction germinates pollination
fruit fertilisation seed flower

The life cycle of a flowering plant has a number of stages. A young plant develops when a seed _____.

The plant matures until it produces a _____, which has several parts adapted for _____.

Male sex cells are transferred to the female part of the flower during the process of _____.

These sex cells join with female sex cells at _____. Following this process the ovary develops into a _____. This contains a _____ and the method for moving it away from the parent plant. This process, which is called _____, requires some help to remove the seed from the parent plant.

2 (a) Explain why seeds are dispersed away from their parent plant.
  (b) Describe three methods by which seeds can be dispersed.

3 Look at the diagram of the sycamore seed earlier in this chapter (in the section called 'Dispersal of seeds and fruits'. Why is it suited to its method of dispersal?

4 Draw a diagram of a seed that would be suited to dispersal by a furry animal. Explain why it is suited to this method of dispersal.

5 Why are fruits such as cherries so brightly coloured and sweet tasting?

6 (a) Draw and label the main parts of a germinating runner bean.
  (b) Explain what a seed needs in order to germinate.

7 Match up the parts of the seed with the job they carry out:

The embryo shoot	provides the first raw materials for the growth of the young plant.
The embryo root	grows into the stem and leaves.
The seed coat	grows to anchor the young plant in the soil and absorb water.
The food store	protects the embryo against drying out and rotting.

6 Healthy living

You have learned that a living organism needs a supply of food and oxygen. These are required to provide the energy needed to keep cells alive and to carry out life processes.

As you know, the heart acts as a pump to move blood around the body. The blood can collect food from the gut and oxygen from the lungs and then take both the food and oxygen to the cells.

The human body is very good at carrying out life processes and a human can stay alive despite many problems. However, for a human to stay fit and keep healthy she/he should:

- eat a balanced diet (see Chapter 2)
- take a regular amount of exercise
- take no unnecessary health risks.

Exercise is good for you

An animal needs energy to be able to move. The movement could be as simple as lifting an arm up and down, or as energetic as running a marathon. Indeed, any amount of exercise will mean that the muscle cells need to be given more energy.

Energy is provided by food and oxygen. There is a kind of 'burning' process that lets out the energy that is stored in food. During exercise more and more energy is needed, so more food and oxygen must be delivered to the muscle cells. The way this happens is shown in the following diagram.

By breathing faster and deeper you can get four or five times more oxygen into the blood than you do when you are resting.

Measuring exercise

As you exercise, the heart has to beat faster and faster to pump more blood around the body in order to deliver more oxygen to the muscles. Your heart rate changes during exercise; it rises when you are doing a lot and begins to return to normal (resting heart rate) when you stop.

In fit people (people who exercise often) the resting heart rate is slower than that in unfit people, and after exercise their heart rate returns to resting much more quickly than in unfit people.

You can measure someone's heart rate by taking their **pulse**. This involves feeling for pulsations in an artery close to the surface of the skin; such as in the wrist. The pulses of blood occur every time the heart beats.

Heart beats **faster** to pump more blood to the muscles. The blood carries oxygen and food.

Lungs breathe **deeper** and **faster** so more oxygen can pass into the blood (and more carbon dioxide can be breathed out).

Investigation: Measuring your heart rate (pulse) during and after exercise

You can measure the changes in your pulse rate during and after exercise as shown.

The aim of this experiment is to investigate how exercise affects the rate at which the heart beats.

Good places for taking a pulse are:
• just in front of the ear, under the jaw
• at the wrist.

The number of beats in 15 seconds can be counted. Then the pulse rate = number counted x 4 (in beats per minute).

Caution: you should not carry out this form of exercise if you have a health problem or if you are recovering from an illness. Ask your teacher if you are not sure.

In this investigation you will measure your recovery rate following a set amount of exercise. You should carry out the test with a partner – one person carries out the exercise while the other does the timing and recording. The exercise involves stepping on and off a low stool or step 30 times per minute (so each step up and down should take 2 seconds).

- Step up and down for 5 minutes.
- Sit down and rest for 1 minute.
- Measure and work out the pulse rate in beats per minute. Call this pulse rate A.
- Rest for 30 seconds more.
- Measure and work out the pulse rate in beats per minute. Call this pulse rate B.
- Rest for 30 seconds more.
- Measure and work out the pulse rate in beats per minute. Call this pulse rate C.
- Now add together A + B + C.

You can make an assessment of your fitness using this table. The table has been produced for young people up to about 16 years of age.

	Boy	Girl
Very fit	350 or less	380 or less
Quite fit	Approximately 400	Approximately 440
Rather unfit	Approximately 430	Approximately 470
Very unfit	Approximately 460	Approximately 500

1 (a) If this test is to be reliable, certain features of the test must be controlled. Suggest what they are.

(b) Which organ of the body is being tested during this exercise?

2 Apart from fitness level there are other events that may affect the pulse rate. One of these is shock or fear. A sudden shock or a moment of fear can cause the pulse rate to rise. Explain how this could be an advantage to a human.

> **Did you know?**
>
> A baby's pulse is about twice as fast as a teenager's.
>
> A girl's pulse is about 10–15 beats per minute higher than a boy's on average.
>
> Your pulse can go up to 190–200 beats per minute.

How is exercise good for you?

Remember that the heart is made of muscle and because exercise makes the heart beat faster, it actually increases the **fitness** of the heart muscle. This means that regular exercise gives you a 'fitter' heart. You are much less likely to suffer a heart attack if you take regular exercise.

Exercise benefits your health in other ways too:

- It **reduces obesity** because it uses up food reserves and reduces the chance of becoming overweight. Obesity (which is defined as being so overweight that your health is affected) can be very harmful. For example, the extra weight can cause damage to your joints and make it difficult to breathe freely. Obese people are also more likely to develop type 2 diabetes.
- It **increases stamina** because it trains the heart and lungs to deliver more oxygen to the working muscle cells. This means that a fit person can work for longer periods without causing damage to the body.
- It **increases strength** because the muscles are being trained. Different types of exercise can provide extra strength in different muscles. Lifting weights and swimming are good for the arms, whereas running is more likely to benefit the legs.

> Most people who exercise regularly (three times a week) will notice a difference in strength and stamina after just 4 weeks. Exercise also releases natural chemicals in the brain. These natural chemicals make you feel much better after exercise.

Preliminary knowledge: Health risks

Humans are not all identical to one another. The differences between them could have been inherited from their parents (see Chapter 9) or could be the result of their environment. Some differences may lead to an obvious disease; others may just make us less healthy. We can do nothing about the differences we inherit from our parents but we *can* be careful about our lifestyle. Taking the health risks described in the next section can seriously damage the body and the brain.

Smoking

Smoking tobacco-containing cigarettes can make breathing very difficult. Chemicals in cigarette smoke damage the air sacs in the lungs (see Chapter 3). Emphysema is a condition in which the air sacs are so damaged it becomes very hard to breathe. Some chemicals in cigarette smoke can cause cancer (see Chapter 1), usually of the throat or lungs.

In addition, smoking gives you bad breath and yellows your teeth and fingernails. The nicotine in tobacco smoke is very addictive (see 'What is addiction?' later in this chapter).

Drinking alcohol

Alcohol is a very dangerous **drug** if consumed in large quantities. Even in small amounts it slows down your reactions, impairs your judgement and may cause you to lose a lot of body heat.

In larger amounts, alcohol damages the liver, stomach and the heart. It can make people put on weight as it contains a lot of energy (see Chapter 2) and it can damage their sex organs. Alcohol makes cigarette smoke more likely to cause cancer of the tongue or voice box.

Substance misuse

Solvents and aerosols can be abused by people sniffing and breathing the fumes. Some glue and paint fumes can damage the brain, and aerosols can cause a person to choke and suffocate.

■ There is a health warning clearly displayed on all cigarette packets

■ Alcohol can be very damaging if consumed regularly and in large quantities

6 *Healthy living*

Recreational drugs

Recreational drugs are chemicals, just like the medicines prescribed by a doctor, but they are extremely dangerous to the health and are illegal. Some, like LSD and ecstasy, can damage the brain. Others can make the heart beat dangerously fast. Many drugs sold by dealers are not pure and are mixed with substances that can make people very ill.

As well as the effects on health, recreational drugs can have long-term effects on mental health. The drug marijuana, for example, is known to cause **paranoia** and memory loss.

What is addiction?

Addiction is when you do not have control over doing, taking or using something, to the point where it could be harmful to you or other people. Both smoking and drinking alcohol are addictive.

Many people become addicted to illegal recreational drugs. This means that they cannot carry on their normal lives without the drug.

Addiction can cause very serious changes in behaviour; drug addicts may steal from their friends and family or go without food to buy drugs. Addicts who use needles to inject drugs can also catch blood diseases (HIV infection and hepatitis, for example) from needles they share with other addicts.

Sensible choices

The most important point about all these health risks is that you have control over them. You can make a choice about your lifestyle – remember that you have probably only lived approximately one-seventh of your lifespan. It is possible that even a few uses of drugs can make you become addicted, and eating habits that you start when young can cause problems later in life. What you choose to do now could affect the rest of your life and the lives of your friends and relatives.

Don't forget that even without these additional health risks you will need to eat a balanced diet and take regular exercise.

Exercise 6.1: Healthy living

1 Make a list of the three requirements for a healthy lifestyle.
2 Why is it so difficult to give up smoking?
3 Give three benefits of regular exercise.
4 Match up the following features of lifestyle with the problems they cause:

Smoking	Weakness of muscles
Excessive use of alcohol	Damage to the liver
Addiction to drugs	Obesity
Overeating of fatty foods	Choking to death
Too little exercise	Poor brain development
Breathing aerosols	Lung cancer

Extension questions

5 A student agreed to have his heart rate (pulse rate) measured every five minutes for a period of an hour. The results are shown in the table.

Time/ minutes	0	5	10	15	20	25	30	35	40	45	50	55	60
Pulse rate/ beats per minute	72	72	75	90	107	124	127	111	90	76	72	72	72

   (a) Plot a graph of the results. Put time on the x-axis (along the bottom) and pulse rate on the y-axis (up the side). Put a suitable title on your graph.

   (b) From the graph give:

      (i) the resting heart rate

      (ii) when the student began to take exercise

      (iii) when the student stopped exercising

      (iv) how long the student's pulse took to return to normal.

   (c) Explain why the pulse rate increased during exercise.

6 Use the internet or your library to find out more about the health problems caused by the overuse of alcohol.

Micro-organisms and disease

Many of the life processes in the human body are under a sort of automatic control. These controls keep factors such as body temperature and the concentration of food molecules in the blood within the minimum and maximum levels permitted to keep an organism alive. Sometimes these controls cannot keep up with changes in the body. A person in this situation will show certain **signs** (such as a raised body temperature) and will experience **symptoms** (such as feeling very tired). We would now say that the person is **diseased**.

Classification of diseases

At the simplest level diseases can be classified into two categories: non-infectious and infectious.

- **Non-infectious diseases** cannot be caught from another individual. These diseases may be the result of a number of causes *but do not normally result from the actions of another organism*. Good examples of non-infectious diseases are **heart disease** caused by a very fatty diet (see Chapter 2) or **lung cancer** caused by smoking (see Chapter 3).
- **Infectious diseases** are those that can be caught or passed on from one individual to another. These diseases are caused by some other living organism, usually a micro-organism.

Micro-organisms are living organisms that are too small to be seen with the naked eye. Scientists have discovered many different types of micro-organism (sometimes called **microbes**) by using an instrument called a **microscope** (see Chapter 1). A good microscope can **magnify** a micro-organism to make it look bigger, as well as making its structure look clearer.

These micro-organisms live in the environment but can enter our bodies:

- in food or water
- from the air, such as on droplets from coughs and sneezes
- through a cut or wound
- during sexual intercourse.

Micro-organisms cause disease upon entering the body when they interfere with the way the body works. **Bacteria** and **viruses** are examples of micro-organisms that can cause this kind of problem.

An example of a viral disease is **influenza** or flu. It is spread from one patient to another via coughs and sneezes. People with this disease feel aches and pains, high temperature, headache, tiredness and a sore throat. It is similar to the common cold, which is also caused by a virus, but influenza is more severe and usually lasts longer. Most people recover on their own, but flu can be more serious in the elderly and very young, or those with other medical problems, particularly breathing difficulties, such as asthma (see Chapter 3). In these cases, patients can be given antiviral medication in the form of a flu jab.

An example of a bacterial disease is **tuberculosis** or TB. This is also spread via coughs and sneezes, but usually only after prolonged exposure to someone with the illness. It therefore often spreads within households. Poor living conditions and overcrowding increase the risk of TB, for example in hostels, refuges, prisons and student halls. TB mainly affects the lungs. Patients have a persistent cough, high temperature, tiredness and a loss of appetite. TB is treated with antibiotics (see 'Medicines can help to fight disease', later in this chapter).

Both influenza and TB can be prevented by injection with the appropriate vaccine.

The following diagrams show how viruses and bacteria can cause disease.

Viruses (e.g. influenza, the common cold and Ebola)

- Viruses are very small micro-organisms that only come *alive* when they enter the body.
- They have a simple structure, with just a few genes wrapped in a protein coat.
- They invade and take over the cells of the host (you!) and use your cells to make hundreds of copies of themselves (called replication).
- The damaged cells can make you feel really ill.
- Viruses cannot be controlled by antibiotics.

Protein coat

Genetic material

1 The virus attaches itself to the cell.

2 The virus genes give instructions to the nucleus.

3 The cell then makes many copies of the virus.

4 The cell bursts and viruses escape. They can now invade more cells.

> **Did you know?**
> We sneeze because broken bits of cells irritate the lining of the nose.

Bacteria (e.g. tuberculosis, tetanus and food poisoning)

- Bacteria are smaller than body cells but bigger than viruses.
- They are cells and have a membrane, cell wall, cytoplasm and genes, but no nucleus.
- They can live inside the body or on the skin.
- They grow and reproduce by dividing very quickly, even as often as every 30 minutes.
- When they divide they use up foods that the body cells need. The bacteria can release **toxins** (poisons) that can make you feel very ill.
- Bacteria can be killed by:
  - **antibiotics** inside the body
  - **antiseptics** on the skin
  - **disinfectants** on work surfaces and in toilets.

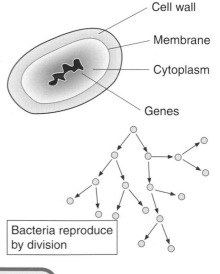

Cell wall

Membrane

Cytoplasm

Genes

Bacteria reproduce by division

> **Did you know?**
> In favourable conditions, and assuming no cell death, one bacterium can divide so many times in 24 hours that the bacterial colony would weigh more than 10 kg (the same as ten standard-sized bags of sugar!).

Defence against disease

The body has several natural defences against disease:

- The **skin** helps to keep micro-organisms away from the body's tissues.
- **Blood clots** stop micro-organisms from entering the body through wounds.
- **White blood cells** engulf (eat) invading micro-organisms, or produce antibodies to destroy them.

The skin is a natural barrier

The skin acts as a barrier to infection by micro-organisms. Even if there are natural gaps in the skin, for example the eyes and ears, the body produces chemicals that help to defend these gaps. The part played by this first line of defence is shown in the following diagram.

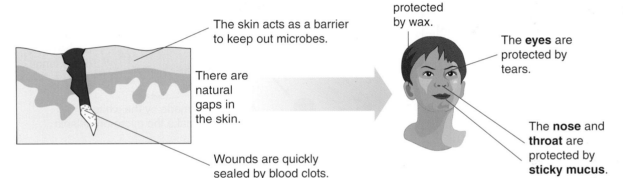

The skin acts as a barrier to keep out microbes.

There are natural gaps in the skin.

Wounds are quickly sealed by blood clots.

The **ears** are protected by wax.

The **eyes** are protected by tears.

The **nose** and **throat** are protected by **sticky mucus**.

■ The skin is the first line of defence

Blood clotting protects open wounds

A blood clot forms when a wound is made in the skin. The clot is started by small pieces of blood cell called **platelets** and completed when red blood cells become trapped by a network of fibres. The blood dries out to form a scab. The scab falls off once the skin beneath it has been repaired. Sometimes a large scab will leave a **scar** when it falls off.

White blood cells help in two different ways

One group of white blood cells, called phagocytes, can find micro-organisms and destroy them directly by eating and digesting them. Sometimes this kills the white blood cells themselves; in fact, the **pus** that sometimes collects near a wound is formed from dead white blood cells.

Another type of white blood cell, called a **lymphocyte**, can recognise micro-organisms and produces special proteins called **antibodies** to fight them. Your body can make a different antibody for every bacterium or virus it meets, and can remember any micro-organisms that have been met in the past. A few of these so-called **memory lymphocytes** are kept for each micro-organism that has ever infected the body so that if the same micro-organism infects you again, the antibodies are made much more quickly. A second infection by the same micro-organism will hardly cause any disease at all. When this happens, scientists say that the body has developed **immunity** to this micro-organism.

The part played by white blood cells in defence against disease is shown in the following diagram.

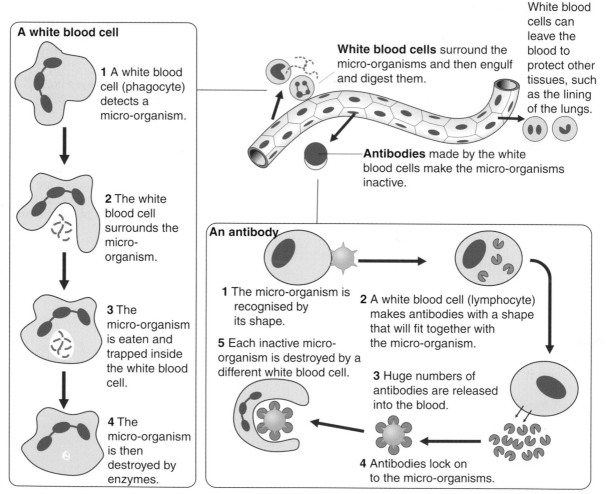

■ White blood cells are the second line of defence

Helping the body to fight disease

The immune system might not be able to work quickly enough to protect the body if it becomes infected by a really dangerous micro-organism. Doctors have developed a method for preparing the immune system for attack by this kind of micro-organism. This kind of protection is called **immunisation** or **vaccination**. The process is outlined in the following diagram.

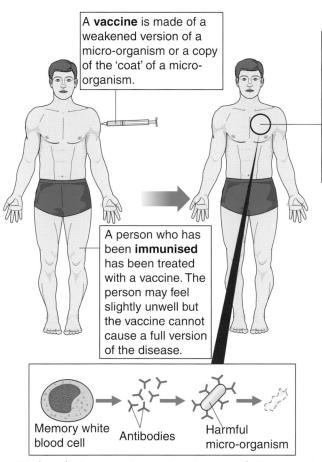

A **vaccine** is made of a weakened version of a micro-organism or a copy of the 'coat' of a micro-organism.

A person who has been **immunised** has been treated with a vaccine. The person may feel slightly unwell but the vaccine cannot cause a full version of the disease.

Memory white blood cell   Antibodies   Harmful micro-organism

- The immunised person now has white blood cells that have been *tricked*. They have made antibodies that can recognise the real micro-organism and **not** just the weakened version.
- Some of these cells are **memory** cells and will be able to make antibodies if the **real** micro-organism infects the body.
- Sometimes a person needs **booster** injections to keep up the number of memory cells.

Edward Jenner

The term vaccination comes from the Latin word for cow (*vacca*). This process was first tried out by a doctor called Edward Jenner in 1796. He found out that the disease cowpox was harmless, but very similar to the deadly smallpox. He injected a small boy called James Phipps with cowpox micro-organisms (he called this process vaccination) and found that it gave the boy protection against smallpox.

Why would Jenner not be allowed to try this out nowadays?

■ Weakened micro-organisms or inactive parts of micro-organisms are used in vaccinations to give us artificial immunity

Did you know?

- A pregnant woman passes antibodies across the placenta. So a newborn baby is already **naturally immunised** to some common illnesses!
- The first breast milk made by the mother is made up of antibodies. The baby's immune system is topped up for the first few days.

Medicines can help to fight disease

Sometimes a disease cannot be prevented by the body's natural defence mechanisms. A person may become ill and need help to recover. A doctor may prescribe a **medicine** to do this. Some useful points to remember:

- It is important to know whether a particular disease is caused by a virus or a bacterium, because this information can help to determine the method of treatment. For example, antibiotics only work against bacteria and do not have any effect on diseases caused by viruses.
- Sometimes a patient can be helped to deal with an illness with **painkillers** such as aspirin or paracetamol. These drugs reduce the body temperature and make the person feel better and this can help them during a period of illness. An overdose of painkillers can be very dangerous; paracetamol, for example, may cause irreversible liver damage.
- A doctor may prescribe drugs to prevent future disease. Aspirin, for example, may reduce the risk of a heart attack or stroke in the future.

Exercise 6.2: Micro-organisms and disease

1 Name one disease that:
   (a) is caused by a virus
   (b) is infectious
   (c) could be caused by a poor diet
   (d) is caused by bacteria
   (e) can result from an unhealthy lifestyle.

2 My mother did not study science. She used to tell me that my body was protected by 'red and white soldiers'. What do you think she meant? Was she correct?

3 Write down two differences between bacteria and viruses.

4 What is an antibiotic? What is the difference between an antibiotic, an antiseptic and a disinfectant?

Extension question

5 Read the description of Jenner's discovery of vaccination and answer the questions that follow it.

Edward Jenner worked in a country town. He noticed that girls who milked cows often caught a disease called cowpox. They had spots on their hands but otherwise were not ill at all. Jenner noted that the girls who caught cowpox never became ill from smallpox, a much more serious disease. Jenner collected the pus from one of the cowpox spots on a milkmaid's hand and scratched the pus into the arm of his nephew (an eight-year-old boy called James Phipps). The boy caught cowpox and felt slightly unwell for a few days but soon recovered. Edward Jenner then transferred pus from a person with smallpox into the arm of James Phipps. James did not catch smallpox and showed no signs of the disease.

(a) What would have happened to James Phipps if Jenner's experiment had not worked?

(b) Use a diagram to explain why James Phipps did not catch smallpox.

(c) Use your library or the internet to find out why people are no longer vaccinated against smallpox.

◯ Individuals and the community can fight disease together

It is important to understand that the fight against disease involves several levels of responsibility.

- The **personal level**: each individual can take responsibility for his or her own social habits.
- The **community level**: local health services must be correctly managed and financed.
- The **worldwide level**: many nations could accept responsibility for setting up and carrying out vaccination programmes.

Personal responsibilities

An individual can reduce his or her chances of contracting some diseases by trying to achieve the following:

- having good **personal hygiene** (see next section)
- eating a **balanced diet** (see Chapter 2)
- taking regular **exercise**
- having sufficient **rest**, since the main production of chemicals controlling growth takes place during sleep, and a rested person is less likely to suffer from an accident
- **not smoking** (see Chapter 3)
- controlling and **limiting alcohol intake**.

■ Looking after your teeth is a very important part of personal hygiene

Personal hygiene

There are a number of important steps to good personal hygiene.

- Washing hair can help to keep bacteria and nits out of your hair.
- Washing underarms stops bacteria feeding on body fluids and creating body odour (BO).
- Washing hands is particularly important, especially after using the toilet and before eating. This reduces the risk of spreading food poisoning.
- Brushing your teeth twice a day can help fight tooth decay.
- Washing and drying feet stops smells and can also stop athlete's foot (a fungal infection).

Regular health check-ups are also very important. Doctors can often spot disease early and treat it very effectively. Opticians and dentists can prevent future problems with your eyes and teeth if visited regularly.

Community responsibilities

Because we often live close together in towns and cities, we share many facilities that affect our health. For these reasons we must accept community responsibilities. These responsibilities include:

- providing a supply of **safe, clean drinking water** to reduce the risk of diseases like cholera and dysentery
- removal of sewage and refuse; this stops unpleasant smells and removes potential breeding grounds for bacteria, flies and rats, all of which can be disease carriers
- providing **medical care** for the unwell to help limit the spread of disease
- keeping a check on standards of health and hygiene, especially in the **preparation of food.**

Worldwide responsibilities

World health programmes organise the provision of drugs and food supplies to poor countries and regions hit by natural disasters or war. They also co-ordinate vaccination programmes, arrange the digging of wells for clean water, and aim to educate people, for example about hygiene, safe medical practices and safe sex.

The largest and most important group is the **World Health Organization (WHO)**. This group aims to raise the level of health of all the citizens of the world so that they can lead socially productive lives.

The WHO has had some great successes:

- **Reduction of the infant death rate**, by providing a better diet for mothers and their infants.
- **Elimination of smallpox**, by a well-co-ordinated vaccination programme.
- **Reduction in malaria**, which affects more than 2 million people a year, by a variety of methods, including the provision of mosquito nets and the draining of swampy areas to reduce the number of mosquitoes, which are the carriers of the disease.
- **Improved supplies of safe water**, by the construction of water-treatment plants.

Together, these combined efforts have made great progress in fighting disease across the world.

Remove rubbish to stop smells and infestations.

Provide clean water to reduce water-borne diseases.

Get rid of sewage to reduce smells and risk of harmful organisms.

■ Community responsibilities

7 Material cycles and energy: photosynthesis

> **Remember:**
> - Plants are living organisms and can carry out all the life processes.
> - Plants must be able to make foods. The foods provide raw materials for growth as well as energy.
> - Plants do not move very much, so they must be able to feed without moving.

Preliminary knowledge: Photosynthesis

Very few plants can trap or catch ready-made food. Instead they must make their own food. They make their food by combining the gas **carbon dioxide** from the air with **water** from the soil. They need **energy** to do this and as you will remember, this energy comes from **sunlight**. The energy in sunlight is trapped by a green pigment, called **chlorophyll**, in the **chloroplasts** of cells in the leaves of the plant.

The method plants use to feed themselves is called **photosynthesis**. The name gives you a clue about what happens during this process. *Photo* means 'using light' and *synthesis* means 'putting together'.

Photosynthesis is summarised by the word equation:

$$\text{carbon dioxide} + \text{water} \xrightarrow[\text{chlorophyll}]{\text{light energy}} \text{glucose} + \text{oxygen}$$
$$\text{(reactants)} \qquad\qquad\qquad \text{(products)}$$

The glucose is usually converted into **starch**. Starch is a larger molecule, made up of many glucose units. It is a more stable and useable molecule for food and energy storage.

The process of photosynthesis therefore provides food for the plant. This food can be used to provide energy that can be stored as starch or used for the growth of the plant. The food that the plant keeps and stores inside its body is called **biomass**. This biomass eventually provides food for many animals.

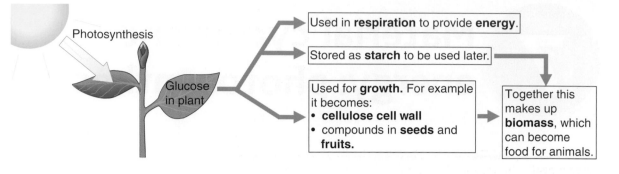

Plants and animals

The biomass of plants provides animals with a useful food supply, which is why many animals eat plants. Sometimes the animal eats the whole plant; sometimes it may just steal the food store. One way or another, all animals depend on plants for their food. This will be studied in more depth in a section on food chains in Chapter 8.

Balancing oxygen and carbon dioxide in the atmosphere

Photosynthesis gives out the gas oxygen as one of its products. All living cells need oxygen to release the maximum amount of energy from food. This is **respiration** (see Chapter 3).

The balance between the processes of photosynthesis and respiration maintains the constant composition of the atmosphere.

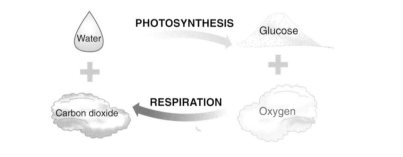

Human activities can affect this balance.

- The burning of fossil fuels uses up oxygen and produces carbon dioxide.
- The cutting down of forests means less photosynthesis, so carbon dioxide levels rise (see the Chapter 8 section, 'Deforestation').

Factors affecting photosynthesis

Any food that the plant has left over, after it has used some for energy, can be used for growing. The plant will be able to grow, so long as it can photosynthesise more than it respires. The four factors that affect photosynthesis are given on the next page.

Did you know?

There are two other types of organism, besides plants, that contain chlorophyll and can make their own food by photosynthesis. These are:

- **algae** – a large and diverse range of organisms, ranging from single-celled algae to different types of seaweed
- **cyanobacteria** – sometimes called blue-green algae, despite being a type of bacteria.

Both of these organisms are usually found in aquatic (water) environments and thus they are an important food source in aquatic food chains.

- **Light intensity:** Light provides the energy needed to join carbon dioxide and water together. The more light there is, the greater the rate of photosynthesis.
- **The level of carbon dioxide:** The air must provide carbon dioxide. There is very little carbon dioxide in the normal atmosphere, so this gas must be replaced quickly by respiration.
- **Temperature:** Thermal energy is needed so that all the chemical reactions in the plant can happen quickly enough. The best temperature for photosynthesis is around 25 °C. Temperatures above 40 °C damage plant cells and photosynthesis comes to a halt.
- **Water:** Water is needed to combine with carbon dioxide and to carry foods around the plant's body. Water is important for photosynthesis but it is not as important as the other factors.

Investigation: Factors affecting photosynthesis – starch detection method

Scientists are very interested in how different factors affect photosynthesis. If they can understand how plants grow, then they may be able to make plants grow more quickly. This could provide more food for humans and other animals.

When a scientist has an idea or prediction that they want to check, they will need to carry out an **experiment**. The idea or prediction is called a **hypothesis**. The experiment must be reliable, or the information it gives will not be useful (see the section on 'Investigations in Science' at the start of this book).

There are a number of different ways in which photosynthesis by the plant can be measured. The easiest method is to show whether or not the plant has been able to make starch. (Remember that you learned about the iodine test for starch in Chapter 2.)

The diagram on the next page outlines the method for showing that light is needed for the production of starch.

This method for detecting photosynthesis is **qualitative**, meaning you can tell whether or not photosynthesis has occurred, but **not** *how much* photosynthesis has occurred.

If the scientist wanted to check how variations in temperature, light, water or carbon dioxide affected the growth of a plant, then it would be necessary to use many plants. The different tests could be carried out on different plants.

1 Describe how you would use this method to investigate the effect of temperature on photosynthesis.
2 Explain why it is important to carry out the tests at the same time on plants that were the same species and the same size at the start of the experiment.

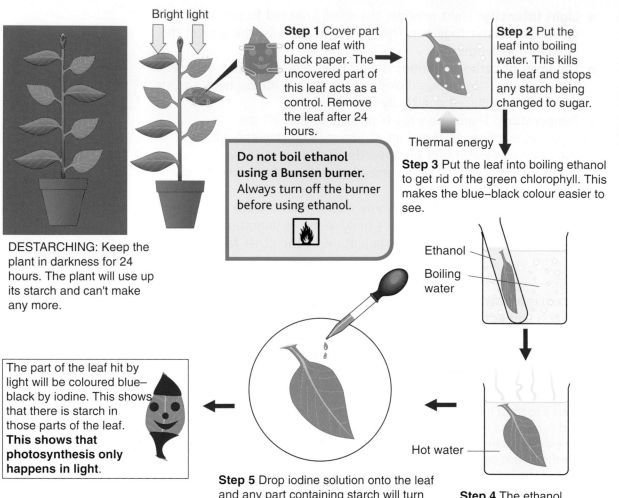

Step 1 Cover part of one leaf with black paper. The uncovered part of this leaf acts as a control. Remove the leaf after 24 hours.

Step 2 Put the leaf into boiling water. This kills the leaf and stops any starch being changed to sugar.

Thermal energy

Do not boil ethanol using a Bunsen burner. Always turn off the burner before using ethanol.

Step 3 Put the leaf into boiling ethanol to get rid of the green chlorophyll. This makes the blue–black colour easier to see.

Ethanol

Boiling water

DESTARCHING: Keep the plant in darkness for 24 hours. The plant will use up its starch and can't make any more.

The part of the leaf hit by light will be coloured blue–black by iodine. This shows that there is starch in those parts of the leaf. **This shows that photosynthesis only happens in light**.

Hot water

Step 5 Drop iodine solution onto the leaf and any part containing starch will turn blue–black. This is a **positive** result. Any parts without starch will be stained brown by the iodine. This is a **negative** result.

Step 4 The ethanol makes the leaf hard, so put it into hot water to soften it.

Investigation: Factors affecting photosynthesis – oxygen production method

In order to measure *how much* or *how fast* photosynthesis is occurring we need a **quantitative** test.

When glucose is produced from carbon dioxide and water during photosynthesis, the gas oxygen is produced as a waste product.

We cannot see oxygen in the atmosphere, but we *can* see oxygen bubbles in water. This is useful for two reasons:

- If we collect the gas as it is produced, we can prove that it is oxygen.
- If we count the bubbles as they are released from the plant, this gives us information about how fast photosynthesis is happening.

The experiment shown in the following diagram explains both of these points.

A stopwatch can be used to count the number of bubbles produced by the plant in a fixed time. This means you can measure the **rate** of oxygen production, which is directly related to the rate of photosynthesis.

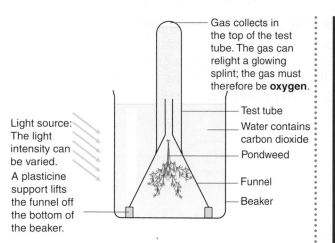

Gas collects in the top of the test tube. The gas can relight a glowing splint; the gas must therefore be **oxygen**.

Light source: The light intensity can be varied.

A plasticine support lifts the funnel off the bottom of the beaker.

Test tube

Water contains carbon dioxide

Pondweed

Funnel

Beaker

In order to make this a **fair test** (see section on 'Investigations in Science'), a scientist wanting to investigate the effect of light intensity on the rate of photosynthesis would set the following parameters:

- Light intensity would be the **independent** (input) variable. Different light intensities could be achieved by moving a light source (such as a lamp) closer to or further away from the plant.
- The rate of oxygen production would be the **dependent** (outcome) variable.
- All other factors would be the **fixed** variables. For example: temperature, the amount of pondweed, the concentration of carbon dioxide.

The experiment would be **repeated** several times to make the results more **reliable**. An **average** result would then be calculated. An average, or **mean**, is calculated by adding together all the data (numbers) and then dividing by the number of data (how many numbers there are).

For example, a student carried out an investigation using the method above to determine the effect of temperature on the rate of photosynthesis. She repeated the experiment five times for two different temperatures and recorded her results in a table.

Temperature/°C	Total number of bubbles released per 10 minutes				
	1	2	3	4	5
20	5	7	6	4	3
35	13	15	16	14	17

She calculated the mean rate of photosynthesis for both temperatures as follows:

- at 20 °C mean = $\dfrac{(5 + 7 + 6 + 4 + 3)}{5}$ = 5 bubbles per ten minutes

- at 35 °C mean = $\dfrac{(13 + 15 + 16 + 14 + 17)}{5}$ = 15 bubbles per ten minutes

1 What was the independent (input) variable in this investigation?
2 What factors would the student have to keep the same (fixed variables) to make this a fair test?
3 What can the student conclude from her results?

Getting it right: growing plants in greenhouses

It is possible to control the process of photosynthesis by growing plants in **greenhouses**. The owner of a greenhouse can control the amount of light, the temperature and the amount of carbon dioxide, as well as making sure that the plants never run out of water.

Exercise 7.1: Photosynthesis

1 During the preparation for the starch test, a leaf is warmed in ethanol. The ethanol turns green. Why is this?

2 A bluebell grows from an underground stem called a bulb. The leaves make glucose and this is stored as starch in the bulb.
   (a) Describe the process by which glucose is made in leaves.
   (b) How could you test to show that starch has been stored in the bulb?
   (c) Bluebells grow in the spring, before most trees have their leaves. Explain why this is the case.

3 Using the apparatus shown earlier in this chapter for collecting gas for measurement (not as a bubble count), two students obtained the following results:
   (a) Plot this information as a line graph.
   (b) At what light intensity did the shoot produce 25 mm³ of oxygen per minute?
   (c) What was the maximum light intensity that seemed to affect the rate of photosynthesis? How could this information be useful to a grower of greenhouse tomatoes?

Light intensity/ arbitrary units	Volume of oxygen released/ mm³ per minute
1	7
2	14
3	21
4	28
5	34
6	39
7	42
8	44
9	45
10	45

4 Copy and complete this table to show that you understand the idea of a fair test.

Factor to be varied	Factor to be measured	Factors to be kept constant
Light	Length of plant	
Amount of carbon dioxide	Length of plant	
Amount of water	Length of plant	
Temperature	Length of plant	

◯ Leaves and roots help plants to grow

So far we have learned that plants need to trap light energy so that they can combine carbon dioxide gas and water into molecules of glucose. They have to do this in order to make the food they require to supply energy and raw materials for growth.

It should not be a surprise to find out that much of the plant's structure is very well adapted to this process. The following diagram illustrates this idea.

Remember:
- Plants make food during a process called photosynthesis.
- Photosynthesis needs carbon dioxide, water and chlorophyll to absorb light energy.

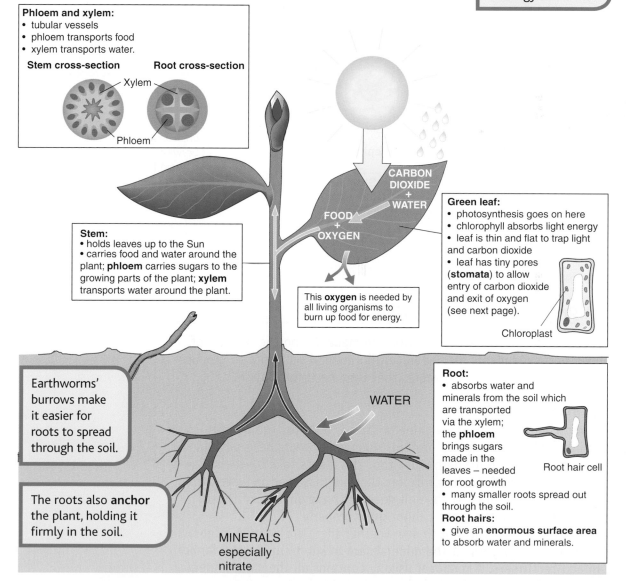

Phloem and xylem:
- tubular vessels
- phloem transports food
- xylem transports water.

Stem cross-section   **Root cross-section**

Xylem

Phloem

Stem:
- holds leaves up to the Sun
- carries food and water around the plant; **phloem** carries sugars to the growing parts of the plant; **xylem** transports water around the plant.

CARBON DIOXIDE + WATER

FOOD + OXYGEN

This **oxygen** is needed by all living organisms to burn up food for energy.

Green leaf:
- photosynthesis goes on here
- chlorophyll absorbs light energy
- leaf is thin and flat to trap light and carbon dioxide
- leaf has tiny pores (**stomata**) to allow entry of carbon dioxide and exit of oxygen (see next page).

Chloroplast

Earthworms' burrows make it easier for roots to spread through the soil.

The roots also **anchor** the plant, holding it firmly in the soil.

WATER

MINERALS especially nitrate

Root:
- absorbs water and minerals from the soil which are transported via the xylem; the **phloem** brings sugars made in the leaves – needed for root growth
- many smaller roots spread out through the soil.

Root hair cell

Root hairs:
- give an **enormous surface area** to absorb water and minerals.

The following diagram shows the structure of a leaf, including stomata, and how water and gases travel through it.

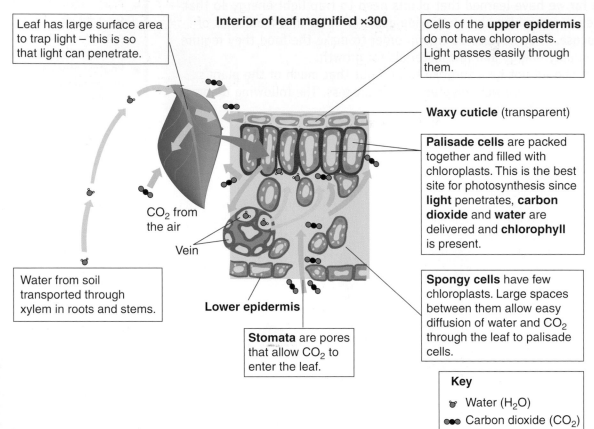

Interior of leaf magnified ×300

Leaf has large surface area to trap light – this is so that light can penetrate.

Cells of the **upper epidermis** do not have chloroplasts. Light passes easily through them.

Waxy cuticle (transparent)

Palisade cells are packed together and filled with chloroplasts. This is the best site for photosynthesis since **light** penetrates, **carbon dioxide** and **water** are delivered and **chlorophyll** is present.

CO_2 from the air

Vein

Spongy cells have few chloroplasts. Large spaces between them allow easy diffusion of water and CO_2 through the leaf to palisade cells.

Water from soil transported through xylem in roots and stems.

Lower epidermis

Stomata are pores that allow CO_2 to enter the leaf.

Key

🐭 Water (H_2O)

●●● Carbon dioxide (CO_2)

⭕ Preliminary knowledge: Minerals

As well as glucose (and starch) that are made during the process of photosynthesis, plants also need certain mineral nutrients to produce some of the other food molecules that they need for growth.

Nitrates and fertilisers

The most important of these mineral salts is **nitrate**. The plant requires nitrate to make its proteins. Remember that these proteins are part of the food for herbivores too. The plants take up their mineral nutrients, including nitrates that are dissolved in water, from the soil via their roots. If the soil does not have enough of these mineral nutrients, the plant cannot grow properly.

Farmers can test the soil to see whether there are enough minerals for their crops to grow. If the minerals are in short supply, the farmer can add **fertilisers**. A fertiliser usually contains all the main minerals that a plant needs, particularly large amounts of nitrate.

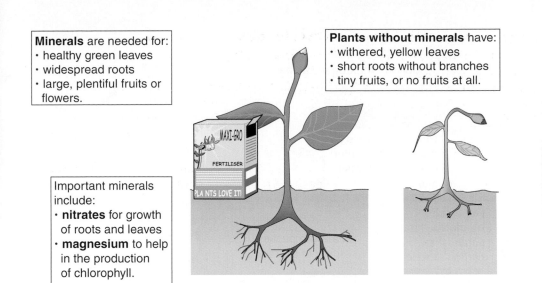

Minerals are needed for:
- healthy green leaves
- widespread roots
- large, plentiful fruits or flowers.

Plants without minerals have:
- withered, yellow leaves
- short roots without branches
- tiny fruits, or no fruits at all.

Important minerals include:
- **nitrates** for growth of roots and leaves
- **magnesium** to help in the production of chlorophyll.

But overuse of fertilisers can cause other problems in the environment. Excess nitrates can be washed out of the soil into lakes and rivers. This can:

- turn rivers green from the growth of algae
- pollute drinking water, which can be especially harmful to babies
- eventually kill off fish and larger animals.

Decomposition and nutrient cycling

So we have learned that plants take carbon dioxide from the air and convert it into glucose by photosynthesis. They also absorb nitrates from the soil and convert them into proteins. This means that the plant has locked up some of the carbon dioxide and nitrate present in the environment. It would not take very long for plants to remove all the carbon dioxide and nitrate from the environment and then no more plants could grow. Since all animals depend on plants for their food (see Chapter 8), if plants cannot grow then animals will die. It is important for the environment that the locked-up nitrate and carbon dioxide are put back into the environment. This is the job of a group of organisms called **decomposers**. These organisms – bacteria and fungi – convert the remains of plants and animals back into these important raw materials. Animals, plants and decomposers are all involved in the natural cycling of the raw materials in the environment. The cycling of carbon dioxide is called the **carbon cycle** and the cycling of nitrates is called the **nitrogen cycle**. Both are described in the following sections.

Cold, acidic and low-oxygen conditions inhibit decomposition. That's why bodies of animals and plants from thousands of years ago are found in peat bogs.

The carbon cycle

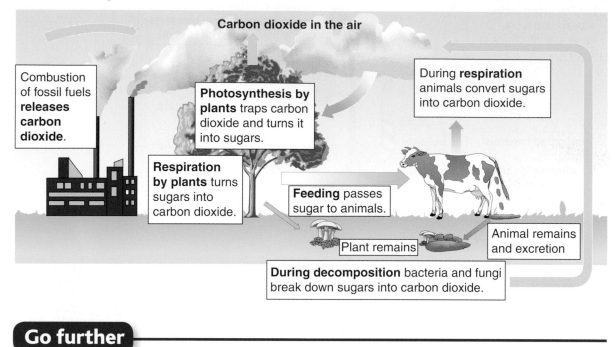

Carbon dioxide in the air

Combustion of fossil fuels **releases carbon dioxide**.

Photosynthesis by plants traps carbon dioxide and turns it into sugars.

During **respiration** animals convert sugars into carbon dioxide.

Respiration by plants turns sugars into carbon dioxide.

Feeding passes sugar to animals.

Plant remains

Animal remains and excretion

During decomposition bacteria and fungi break down sugars into carbon dioxide.

Go further

The nitrogen cycle

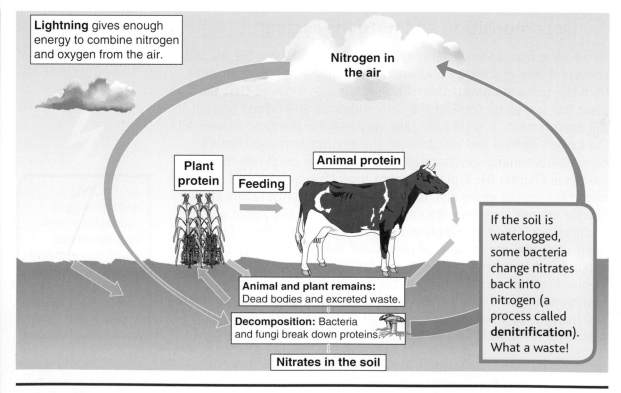

Lightning gives enough energy to combine nitrogen and oxygen from the air.

Nitrogen in the air

Plant protein

Feeding

Animal protein

Animal and plant remains: Dead bodies and excreted waste.

Decomposition: Bacteria and fungi break down proteins.

Nitrates in the soil

If the soil is waterlogged, some bacteria change nitrates back into nitrogen (a process called **denitrification**). What a waste!

Exercise 7.2: Plant nutrition

1 Write down two jobs carried out by the stem of a plant.
2 What is the main job of a leaf? Give two ways in which the leaf is well adapted for this job.
3 Mango trees are grown in hot, dry countries where the soil can be hard and tightly compacted. Farmers water the mango trees by spraying water onto the soil around them.
   (a) (i) a small amount of the water actually reaches the roots of the trees. Suggest one reason why.
       (ii) Suggest one other reason why mango trees do not grow well in soil that is hard and tightly packed.
   (b) Give two reasons why mango trees and other plants need water.
   (c) There is a new method of watering mango trees. Trenches are dug between the trees and filled with small pieces of rock. Plastic pipes with small holes in them are placed on top of the pieces of rock and water is pumped along the pipes. Mango trees watered by this method produce 15% more fruit.

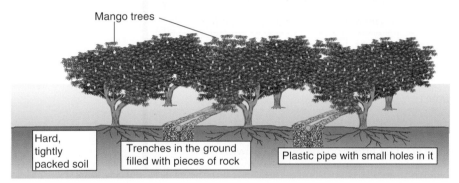

Mango trees

Hard, tightly packed soil

Trenches in the ground filled with pieces of rock

Plastic pipe with small holes in it

   (i) Suggest one reason why pieces of rock are placed in the trenches under the pipes.
   (ii) With the new method, farmers can also add nitrates to the water in the pipes. Give one reason why plants need compounds that contain nitrogen.
4 The drawing shows a plant called *Tillandsia*.

   (a) (i) The leaves of this plant absorb light. Why do plants need light?
       (ii) *Tillandsia* plants grow on the high branches of trees in rainforests. These plants cannot grow well on the lowest branches. Explain why.
   (b) *Tillandsia* plants do not have root hairs on their roots. What two substances do most plants absorb through their root hairs?

(c) Which diagram below shows a root hair?

A   B   C   D

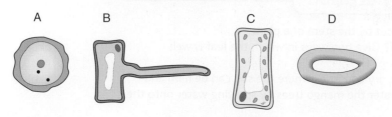

Extension question

5 Five sets of plants were grown. Each one had a slightly different treatment. The plants were weighed after two weeks of growth. How they were treated and how they grew is shown in this table.

Weight/ grams	Treatment
34	Ideal conditions for air, water, light and minerals
32	Ideal conditions for air, water and light **but** only half minerals
18	Ideal conditions for air, water and minerals **but** only half light
28	Ideal conditions for water, light and minerals **but** only half the amount of air
19	Ideal conditions for air, light and minerals, **but** only half the amount of water

(a) Plot the results on a bar chart.
(b) Which treatment had the greatest effect on the plants' growth? Explain why.

8 Relationships in an ecosystem

Remember, all living organisms need a supply of food to carry out their life processes:

- Plants use light energy and chemicals from their surroundings to make their own food.
- Animals cannot *make* their own food but they get their energy and raw materials from the food they eat.
- Decomposers obtain energy and raw materials from the remains of other living organisms.

Animals (and that includes humans) depend on plants for food. Even animals that only eat other animals (carnivores) are dependent on plants, because the animals they feed on are dependent on plants themselves

Preliminary knowledge: Habitats and food chains

Animals and plants live in specific **habitats**. Habitat is a term to describe their local environment. This is a place where a collection of plants and animals live; in other words, where they feed and breed.

Habitats can be any size: from very big, for example rainforests and oceans, to very small, for example a pond, an individual tree or even a single leaf.

Animals and plants in different habitats are suited to survive and thrive in their own particular environment. We call this **adaptation**. For example, a polar bear has a thick layer of fat to keep itself warm in the cold Arctic and cacti plants have swollen stems for storing water in the dry desert.

There may be many different animals and plants in one habitat but they are all linked together by food. We call this an **ecosystem**.

Remember that the feeding links between different organisms make up a **food chain**. A food chain shows how energy and raw materials are passed from one organism to another by feeding.

There are certain rules about food chains:

- They always **start with a green plant** because only green plants can make their own food. Plants make their own food by photosynthesis, so they are called producers.
- Animals eat or consume food, so they are called consumers.
- The arrows in a food chain mean 'food for'. These arrows always point in the direction in which the energy and raw materials are moving as the organisms feed.

> Don't forget that dead leaves, fallen branches and rotten fruits **all** came from plants.

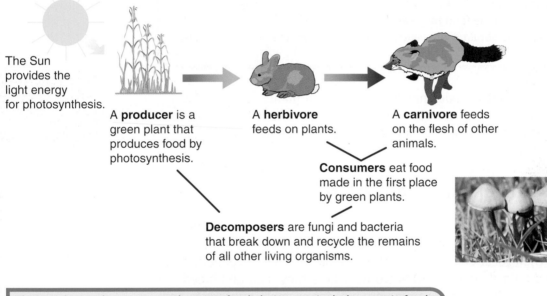

The Sun provides the light energy for photosynthesis.

A **producer** is a green plant that produces food by photosynthesis.

A **herbivore** feeds on plants.

A **carnivore** feeds on the flesh of other animals.

Consumers eat food made in the first place by green plants.

Decomposers are fungi and bacteria that break down and recycle the remains of all other living organisms.

> Algae and cyanobacteria can also start food chains, particularly aquatic food chains. Both these types of organisms create their own food using light energy and chlorophyll. Seaweed, for example, is actually a type of algae, not a plant, and starts most marine (sea) food chains.

There are different types of consumers

Because animals cannot make their own food, they must obtain their food by eating other organisms. Animals are very well adapted to the type of food they eat. Some animals are called **herbivores** because they eat plants (*herba* means 'plant' or 'grass' in Latin). Other animals are called **carnivores** because they eat meat (*caro/carnis* means 'meat' in Latin). Some animals get the best of both worlds; they eat plants *and* meat. These animals are called **omnivores** (*omni* means 'all' in Latin).

Before you move on, make sure you can name an example of a herbivore, a carnivore and an omnivore.

Animals that eat other animals are called predators and the animals that they catch are called prey.

Decomposers

Some micro-organisms (bacteria and fungi) feed on the remains of dead plants and animals or the waste that animals produce. These micro-organisms are decomposers (see Chapter 7 – carbon and nitrogen cycles). Every habitat needs decomposers so that supplies of minerals and other food materials can be recycled.

All change

If one organism in a food chain is affected in some way, then other organisms in the same food chain will also be affected. One example is shown in the following diagram.

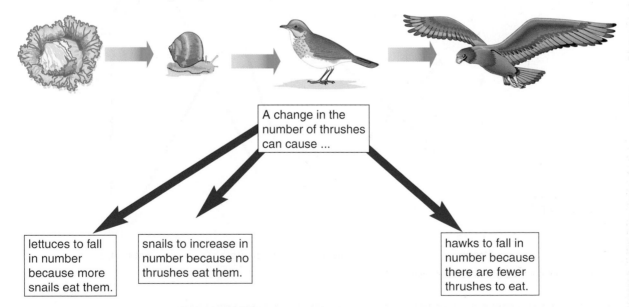

A change in the number of thrushes can cause ...

lettuces to fall in number because more snails eat them.

snails to increase in number because no thrushes eat them.

hawks to fall in number because there are fewer thrushes to eat.

Organisms are less likely to be affected if they can feed on more than one kind of food – in other words, if they can take part in more than one food chain.

Food webs

Most animals and plants actually play a part in more than one food chain. Feeding relationships in a habitat are in fact very complex because food chains overlap. These interlinked food chains are called **food webs**.

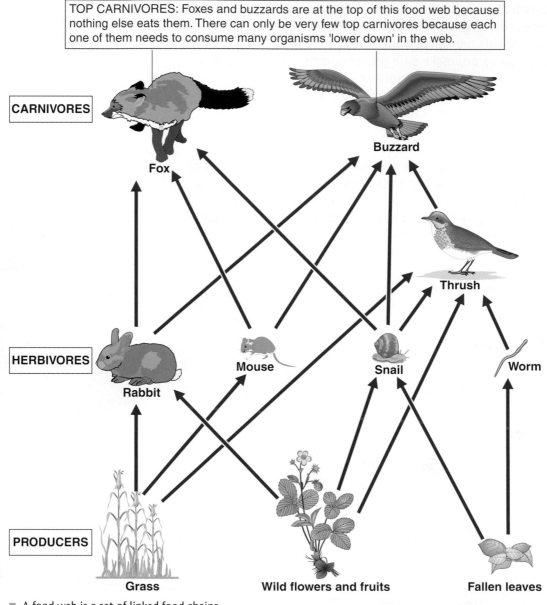

TOP CARNIVORES: Foxes and buzzards are at the top of this food web because nothing else eats them. There can only be very few top carnivores because each one of them needs to consume many organisms 'lower down' in the web.

CARNIVORES

Fox

Buzzard

Thrush

HERBIVORES

Rabbit

Mouse

Snail

Worm

PRODUCERS

Grass

Wild flowers and fruits

Fallen leaves

■ A food web is a set of linked food chains

When you are drawing a food web, arrange all the producers on one level, the herbivores in a second level, and so on. These are called **feeding levels**. This makes it easier to pick out the food chains.

There are advantages in using food webs rather than food chains:

- Food webs give a more realistic picture of the feeding relationships in a habitat. For example, the diagram shows that a fox can feed on more than one kind of herbivore and that grass is eaten by more than one kind of consumer.
- They show how many animals can survive changes in their environment. For example, cold weather might reduce the number of earthworms and snails available to a thrush but it can feed itself on grass seeds and fruits.

Affecting food webs

Removing just one organism from a food web can have many effects because the organism may be involved in many food chains.

The numbers of predators and their prey depend on each other. For example, if there are a lot of foxes (predators) in one habitat, then the rabbit (prey) numbers will quickly fall. If the number of rabbits falls, then there may not be enough food for all the foxes. Some of the foxes will die unless they move to a place where there is more food, or learn to eat other things. In Britain, many foxes have moved into cities where they have learned to feed on food thrown away by humans.

The same thing can happen with insects. Greenfly can breed very quickly if the weather is warm and moist. There can be millions of them in one garden, much to the horror of gardeners. However, a plague of greenfly is a heavenly situation for the animals that love to eat them, such as ladybirds. The ladybird numbers increase and, because there are so many of them, the number of greenfly falls again. There is a cycle between the numbers of predators and their prey.

Taking top consumers (predators) away from a habitat can be particularly dangerous, as the number of herbivores (prey) can increase quickly. This increase in herbivores might mean more producers (plants) are eaten, which in turn means there are fewer producers to trap light energy. This can all lead to a rapid breakdown of the whole food web.

> Don't forget – there must always be more prey than predators!

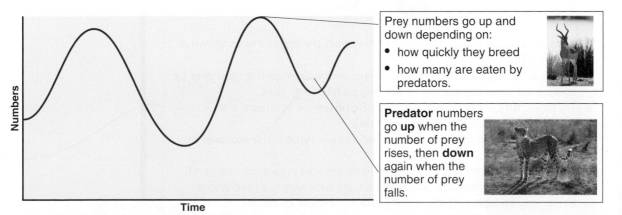

Prey numbers go up and down depending on:
- how quickly they breed
- how many are eaten by predators.

Predator numbers go **up** when the number of prey rises, then **down** again when the number of prey falls.

■ The relationship between predators and prey

Adding a new organism to a food web can be just as dangerous as taking one away. Rats were introduced to the islands of New Zealand when they escaped from ships stopping to take on food and water. The rats killed off many ground-nesting birds. The situation was made worse when stoats were introduced to try to kill off the rats. The stoats also killed and ate the ground-nesting birds. The conservation of wild organisms is a very complicated business and should be left to expert biologists (see the section on conservation later in this chapter).

Investigation: Study of a food chain in a local habitat

Different organisms in a habitat are linked to one another by **feeding**. The feeding links between different organisms in a habitat make up a **food chain**. The aim of this investigation is to study a food chain in a local habitat to determine the relationships present. If some of the organisms from a habitat are collected they can be examined and placed into one of the groups that make up a food chain.

Small organisms can be collected from a sample of leaf litter, for example. The organisms can be collected using some form of Tullgren funnel, as shown below.

Heat and light source, e.g. lamp

Leaf litter

Filter mesh

Funnel

Animals move down

Collecting pot

- Collect a sample of leaf litter, and then extract the organisms as shown in the diagram.
- Examine the organisms, using a hand lens or simple magnifier: you **may** be able to see some adaptation to feeding, such as large jaws.
- Try to identify the organisms as far as 'herbivore' or 'carnivore' – your teacher will be able to help you with this.
1 Arrange the organisms into a simple food chain. What is the producer in this food chain?
2 Question 3 in Exercise 8.1 will help you to see how organisms in a pond can be arranged into food chains and a food web. Why is a food web a better way to represent the feeding relationships in a habitat?

Exercise 8.1: Food chains

1 Think of a habitat within your school grounds. Identify and write down a food chain from this habitat.

2 Give an example of a herbivore, a carnivore and an omnivore that would live in a hedgerow or woodland habitat. Name one decomposer and explain why it is so important in this habitat.

Extension question

3 Some students made a survey of a freshwater pond. After many visits they put together their results in this list:

- Hydra feeds on water fleas.
- Diving beetles feed on water fleas and on mayfly larvae.
- Pond snails feed on algae and on pondweed.
- Pond skaters feed on water fleas and tadpoles.
- Perch feed on tadpoles, diving beetles, water fleas and pond skaters.
- Herons feed on perch.
- Mayfly larvae feed on algae.
- Water fleas feed on algae.
- Tadpoles feed on algae and on water fleas.

(a) Use this information to construct a food web for this pond.

(b) What is the top consumer for this food web?

(c) What happens to the animals and plants that die before they are eaten?

(d) Choose one food chain from your food web. Research what a 'pyramid of numbers' is and draw one that you would expect for this food chain.

Conservation

Humans may cause damage to the environment (this is what we mean by **pollution**), but they can also do good things to the environment. Many people are now involved in **conservation**. Conservation involves looking for ways to protect the environment.

Before we look at some of the ways in which we can preserve the environment, let's look at how it can be destroyed. The diagram on the next page shows how humans have been responsible for cutting down huge numbers of trees (**deforestation**) over much of the Earth's surface.

In comparison to this, humans have also set up schemes for the large-scale planting of trees (**reforestation**). Large numbers of trees may be planted in areas that had previously been cleared or that are thought likely to benefit from tree cover. For example, millions of trees were planted when the M25 motorway around London was built.

Soil fertility is reduced
- Trees contain most of the forest's minerals and when trees are cut down and taken away, the minerals can't be recycled.
- Wind and water can cause soil erosion, because the tree roots aren't there to bind the soil together.

Flooding and landslides
- Once trees are cut down, they cannot absorb water. Heavy rainfall is not absorbed and can result in flooding and landslides from steep hillsides.

Changes to the atmosphere
Fewer trees mean:
- **more carbon dioxide** because the gas is not absorbed for photosynthesis
- **less oxygen** because it is not produced by photosynthesis
- **drier air**, because there are fewer leaves to give out water.

Extinction of species
For example:
- The mountain gorilla depends on the rain forest for its habitat.
- Osprey depend on pine forests for nesting.
- **Many plants provide medicines,** e.g. contraceptive chemicals, anti-cancer drugs and painkillers.

■ Deforestation is a disaster

■ Even nature reserves can be cut down for road building!

There are a number of reasons for carrying out these programmes:

- The trees may be a valuable cash crop, providing timber for building purposes (as with many of the coniferous plantations in this country) or for fuel (as with the quick-growing eucalyptus trees, which are planted in Central Africa).
- The trees may help to reverse soil erosion and are particularly valuable in areas that have become deserts.
- The forests may be valuable wildlife habitats. For example, red squirrels, which have reduced in numbers in the UK, can thrive in Scots pine plantations (see 'The red squirrel in Britain' later in this chapter).
- The forests may be valuable recreational areas, providing opportunities for leisure activities, such as camping, mountain-biking and orienteering.

Scientists believe that one plant and one animal species become extinct every 30 minutes due to deforestation.

In a well-managed forest all these requirements can be met. Indeed, the Forestry Commission in the UK *must* take all these into account when managing its plantations.

Forests in Britain are a good example of **sustainable development**. Sustainable development means that we should *not* take too much from our environment now, because it will affect its value *for future generations*. Forests with a single species of tree may be very good for growing wood for building or for paper manufacture, but they are:

- very likely to be damaged by pests (a pest does not have far to go to find another tree of the same type)
- very limited in value to wildlife because there is not a great variety of food
- often very boring to look at.

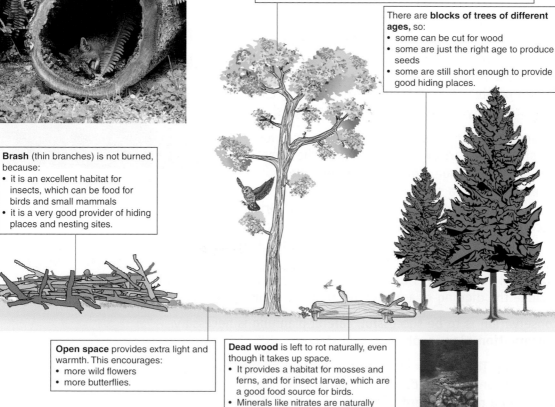

Deciduous trees are planted along the edges of forests that are grown to provide wood for paper or for building.
- They improve the appearance of the woodland, so visitors are happier.
- They provide seeds used as food by wildlife.
- Many insects live in this kind of tree, so there's a greater variety of food for different species of wildlife.
All this helps to save wildlife for the future.

There are **blocks of trees of different ages,** so:
- some can be cut for wood
- some are just the right age to produce seeds
- some are still short enough to provide good hiding places.

Brash (thin branches) is not burned, because:
- it is an excellent habitat for insects, which can be food for birds and small mammals
- it is a very good provider of hiding places and nesting sites.

Open space provides extra light and warmth. This encourages:
- more wild flowers
- more butterflies.

Dead wood is left to rot naturally, even though it takes up space.
- It provides a habitat for mosses and ferns, and for insect larvae, which are a good food source for birds.
- Minerals like nitrates are naturally returned to the soil.

■ Sustainable development

It *is* possible to use biological knowledge carefully in the management of forests. A forest can provide wood for now and wood and wildlife for the future.

The diagram on the previous page suggests that human effects on the environment may not always be negative ones. We sometimes believe that humans only cause harm to the environment, but there are growing numbers of conservationists who are looking for ways to **manage** the environment. Conservationists try to balance the human demands on the environment with the need to maintain wildlife habitats. This is an important part of sustainable development.

Why is conservation necessary?

The competition between humans and other living organisms means that many species have disappeared completely or fallen in number.

Conservationists therefore really have two jobs:

- they must try to slow down or stop the fall in biodiversity (the number of different species)
- they must try to make the **public aware** of the need to maintain species and their habitats.

What is conservation?

Conservation always involves some form of **management** and almost always involves a balance. For example, a farmer might be encouraged to replant hedgerows but must still be able to make a profit from growing crops. Conservation may involve a number of strategies.

■ This former quarry is being turned into a large pond habitat

- **Preservation:** In its strictest sense this involves keeping some part of the environment the same, without any change. This *might* be possible in an enormous area such as Antarctica but is of less significance in a densely populated area like Britain.
- **Reclamation:** This involves the restoration of damaged habitats. It might include the replacement of grubbed-out hedgerows or the recovery of former industrial sites.
- **Creation:** This involves the production of new habitats. It might include the digging of a garden pond or the planting of a forest.

If conservation is to be successful, careful planning is necessary. A **conservation plan** involves several stages:

- **Sampling:** The number of organisms present at the start of the conservation work needs to be counted (see later in this chapter).
- **Devising a management plan:** This involves considerable biological knowledge; for example, trying to increase the population size of a species will involve knowing what its breeding requirements are.

- **Carrying out the plan**: This will probably involve cost to the conservation organisation involved in the work. Many people become involved in voluntary work, which reduces the financial cost of conservation work.
- **Resampling**: The number of the conserved species needs to be counted again, otherwise the conservationists won't know whether or not their plan has worked. This might be five or ten years after the first sampling if the organism is a slow-breeding species.

Two examples of conservation work are described in the next section. The first example involves the red squirrel, which has become endangered in Britain in recent years. Some scientists suggest it may even be heading for extinction. Suggestions for its conservation largely involve careful **habitat management**. The second example concerns **zoos**, which are extremely popular in many countries. Zoo managers now stress the importance of zoos in conservation rather than as places of entertainment.

The red squirrel in Britain

The red squirrel (*Sciurus vulgaris*) used to be very widespread in Britain, but in most areas it has now been replaced by the larger grey squirrel *(Sciurus carolinensis)*, which was introduced into Britain from North America. There are a number of possible reasons for the decline of the red squirrel.

- **Competition with the grey squirrel**: The red squirrel feeds on conifer seeds from pine cones and eats very little of other foods, such as acorns, fruits and berries. The grey squirrel can survive on a very monotonous diet of a wider range of foods. For example, it can cope with a diet that is almost completely acorns. In a broad-leaved (deciduous) woodland the greys can always find something to eat, especially as they are more willing to feed at ground level and can take advantage of food sources that the more tree-loving reds would ignore.
- **Disease**: It is believed that the grey squirrel carries a virus that usually only causes disease and death in red squirrels. Thus in mixed populations the reds are at a disadvantage.

■ In recent years the red squirrel (top) has been replaced by the larger grey squirrel (bottom)

- **Habitat loss:** Although the red squirrel survives better in coniferous forest, it must have access to trees of different ages to provide food throughout the year. In many recent forest plantings, the trees are all the same age and are largely Sitka spruce, which produces small seeds that are shed early in the year, leaving little food for the reds in the winter.

Conservation plans to support red squirrel numbers must take all of these points into account. One very important point to note is that the introduction of a species from another country is often the cause of problems for native wildlife!

Elimination of competitors
- poison or shoot them; or
- use a chemical to sterilise them (this is a good solution because it doesn't actually kill any animals).

Habitat management
Choose tree species that provide food for red squirrels, e.g. birch. Remove oak and beech because these provide food for grey squirrels. Good conifers include Scots pine because these provide seeds very late in the year for red squirrels.

Habitat management
Red squirrel reserves should be surrounded by at least 3 km of conifer forest or open land to stop entry by grey squirrels.

Supplementary feeding
Selective hoppers have been developed that only allow access to red squirrels. These are placed in clusters of 2 or 3, 20 to 30 metres apart, and filled with a mixture of yellow maize, wheat, peanuts and sunflower seeds. They have the disadvantage that they must be visited regularly and frequently filled.

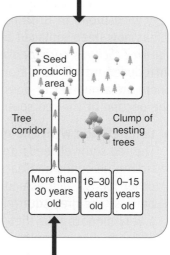

Reintroduction of red squirrels
Small numbers might be released to test the success of habitat management techniques. Survival and behaviour of the introduced reds would be carefully monitored by radio and regular observation.

Forestry practice
The forest should be managed to provide both food and shelter. This typically involves a structure where 30% of trees are 0 to 15 years old, 30% are 16 to 30 years old and 40% are more than 30 years old.
When tree felling, some single seed-producing trees should be left in small groups, in order to provide nesting sites.
Seed-producing areas should be connected by corridors of trees to prevent isolation and make movement between them easier for red squirrels.

■ Saving the red squirrel. The key to successful conservation in this case seems to be the management of a habitat that provides food.

Zoos and conservation

Zoos, or zoological gardens, are areas of confinement for keeping animals in captivity. For many people the fact that the animals *are* in captivity means that zoos can never be justified – these people say that the animals are being exploited for the amusement of humans. Other people have a different point of view and suggest that without zoos, many species would be extinct. For example, there are more Siberian tigers in zoos than there are in the wild. The supporters of zoos argue that animals can be bred in zoos until their habitat is secured for their eventual release. The anti-zoo people argue back that breeding animals in captivity is breeding animals for captivity, and point out that reintroduction to the wild is very rarely successful.

Zoo visits are extremely popular. In the United States more people visit zoos than visit Disneyland. It is extremely important to note that zoo directors justify keeping large, attractive animals because they say that these species generate income that can then be used to conserve less glamorous species. Tigers, pandas and elephants are examples of these **flagship** species. Many zoo visitors will contribute money to conserve elephants, but this money also conserves those species that live in the same habitat as the elephant. Some of the possible benefits of zoos to conservation are explained below.

Good points

Animals get food and shelter and are looked after by a vet.

Animals may breed, which is important in preserving endangered species.

People enjoy visiting zoos. Entry fees can be spent on animals' welfare and people may give money for conservation work.

Zoos may get people interested in animals and conservation.

Bad points

Animals may not have mates for breeding.

Animals may be in the wrong groups, for example, wolves like to live in packs.

Cages may be small so animals get bored.

Zookeepers may not be able to provide food that the animals are used to.

Throughout these sections on pollution and conservation you should be able to see how humans have the potential to alter their environment. It is vital that future generations of scientists use this power carefully, that they live up to the name *Homo sapiens* – the 'wise man' – if the Earth is to remain habitable for other species as well as our own.

Exercise 8.2: Conservation

1 Find a book or a website about the conservation of a particular species. Try to find an example of an animal or a plant in Britain that has been protected by conservation work. (If you can't find one, try the red kite or the lady's slipper orchid.) Present your findings to the rest of the class.

2 Find a zoo's website. What can you find out about the conservation work of this zoo? Is it ethically wrong to keep animals in zoos? Write a short report of your findings and discuss the pros and cons, including ethical issues, of the zoo's work.

Extension questions

3 Read the following passage carefully and then answer questions (a) to (d).

Between 1947 and 1963 hedges were being removed at an average rate of over 3000 miles per year. This increased to 5000 miles per year by 1968.

A recent report claims that between 1980 and 1985, 5000 miles of hedgerow were removed and 2500 miles were planted in England and Wales.

Older hedges generally provide a richer habitat with a wider variety of plants and animals.

Both during and after the Second World War (1939–45), farmers were encouraged to grow more food, to do so more efficiently and at less cost.

On one Devon farm with small fields, removing 1 mile of hedges provided another 3 acres of arable land and reduced by one-third the average time taken to harvest a field of cereal crops.

In 1987, British tax payers spent about £1 578 000 000 to buy and store surplus UK farm produce.

In the European Economic Community, stored surplus food includes 1 500 000 tonnes of beef.

Farmers are now being encouraged by the European Community to grow less food.

Source: adapted from the Nature Conservancy Council publication, *Points of View No. 1: Hedgerows.* © Crown copyright.

(a) What was the highest average rate of removal of hedges in 1969?

(b) If that rate of hedge removal had continued, what effect would it have had on the variety of wild animals and plants in the countryside and the amount of arable land for farming?

(c) How did the **removal** of hedges per year differ in the period between 1980 and 1985 from that in 1968?

(d) Why is it less important now to gain extra arable land than it was immediately after the Second World War?

Read the following and answer question **(e)**.

A   *Hedges provide an important habitat for wildlife that can help with pollination and biological control.*

B   *Hedges can provide a home for weeds, insect pests, rabbits and crop diseases.*

C   *Hedges take up space that could be planted with crops.*

D   *Hedges are an attractive feature in the rural landscape.*

E   *Expensive labour is needed to maintain hedges.*

F   *Hedges provide a wind break for crops, shelter and shade for farm animals and a barrier to the spread of disease.*

G   *Hedges shade part of the crop, which reduces yield.*

H   *Hedges help to prevent topsoil from blowing away.*

I   *Hedges provide cover for game, such as pheasants and partridges.*

J   *Hedges obstruct the efficient use of modern farm machinery.*

Source: adapted from the Nature Conservancy Council publication, Points of View No. 1: Hedgerows. © Crown copyright.

(e) Choose five statements from the list above to support a case against the removal of hedges.

4 Read the following and then answer the questions **(a)** to **(e)** on the next page.

The publication of newspapers uses up an enormous quantity of paper every day. Paper is manufactured from wood. Large numbers of trees are cut down every year to provide the raw material for the paper industry.

Timber is a very important natural resource. In terms of conservation, it would be helpful if used paper could be collected and repulped. The organisation, collection and sorting of waste paper is an expensive process. As a result very little paper is recycled.

Trees cut down for use must be replaced. The planting of trees to replace those felled is called reforestation. Schemes of reforestation must be established and well managed if supply is to keep up with demand. The quicker-growing tree species are the conifers (softwoods), such as pine and spruce. These are grown over large areas of land, producing forests with relatively few species but giving high productivity quickly and are, therefore, an attractive investment.

There is also a need for the deciduous hardwoods, such as oak and beech. These are much slower growing, taking longer to establish and are therefore, in the short term, a less attractive crop. As a habitat, a mixed deciduous woodland will support a greater variety of species than a conifer plantation.

(a) How does the publication of newspapers affect the world's timber resources?

(b) What do the terms recycling and reforestation mean?

(c) **(i)** Name one coniferous tree.

 (ii) Name one hardwood tree.

(d) How do coniferous woodlands differ from deciduous ones as commercial crops and as habitats for wildlife? Support your answer with reasons.

In overcoming one problem, reforestation schemes may produce secondary conservation problems. More and more frequently large areas of moorland, important habitats themselves, are being used as sites for conifer plantations.

(e) What could happen to Britain's moorland habitats and communities if reforestation schemes were allowed to go on unchecked?

◯ Populations and competition

A **population** is the number of organisms of the same **species** living in the same habitat at the same time. The size of a population does not remain the same from day to day or from year to year. Whether a population gets larger, smaller or stays the same depends on the balance between several different processes. These processes affect whether organisms join the population (making it get bigger) or leave it (making it get smaller). These processes are described in the following diagram.

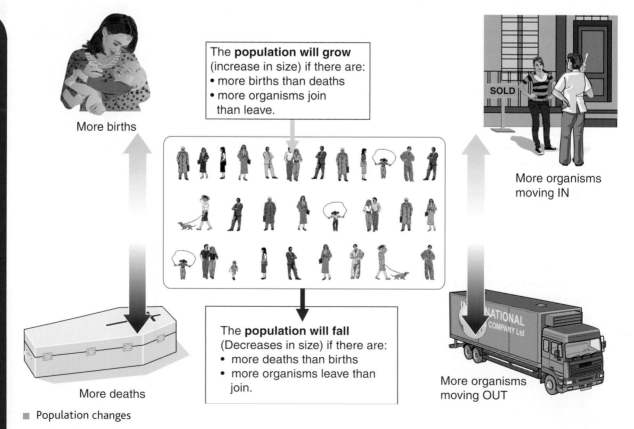

More births

The **population will grow** (increase in size) if there are:
• more births than deaths
• more organisms join than leave.

More organisms moving IN

The **population will fall** (Decreases in size) if there are:
• more deaths than births
• more organisms leave than join.

More deaths

More organisms moving OUT

■ Population changes

This equation should help you remember the factors that affect population growth:

population change = **(number of births + number moving in)** − **(number of deaths + number moving out)**

Counting living organisms

Biologists who are interested in populations can count the number of organisms in an area at a particular time. It would be very difficult and would take too long to count every individual organism of that species, so biologists take a **sample** of the population. Taking samples has several advantages:

■ You might have problems counting these organisms!

● It is much quicker than trying to count every individual.
● It does much less damage to the environment.

One simple way to take a sample is to use a quadrat. A quadrat is a square, usually made of wood or metal, which can be placed on the ground where the organisms are living. The diagram below shows how biologists use quadrats in sampling a population.

| A **quadrat.** Place this in the habitat. | Count the number of organisms of a particular species inside the quadrat. | Work out how many quadrats fit into the habitat. *Now calculate how many organisms are in the whole of the habitat.* |

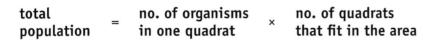

■ Measuring population using a quadrat

The population is then calculated using this equation:

total population = **no. of organisms in one quadrat** × **no. of quadrats that fit in the area**

Reliable results

Living organisms do not spread out equally through their environment. There may be more of one species in one part of the habitat than in another, so a single quadrat might give unreliable results. The biologist should count the number of organisms in several quadrats (probably ten is best) and then find out the average (mean) number in one quadrat. Using this mean value will give a much more reliable count of the population.

To get an average (mean):

● first count the organisms in ten quadrats
● then divide the total number by 10.

You do this because an average (mean) value gives a more reliable result.

Investigation: Using a quadrat to estimate population size

The aim of this investigation is to use a **quadrat** to estimate the population of a plant species in a given area. Your teacher will choose an appropriate species and an area of your location for you to survey. For example, dandelions or daisies on your school field.

● Working in small groups, lay out a string marker (or tape measure) at right angles along two edges of the area you are surveying. The area you will survey measures 5 m by 5 m (25 m²).
● One student should pick a division number on one string at random, and other student should pick a division number on the other string at random.
● Lay the 0.5 m² quadrat over the centre of the place where the two points intersect.

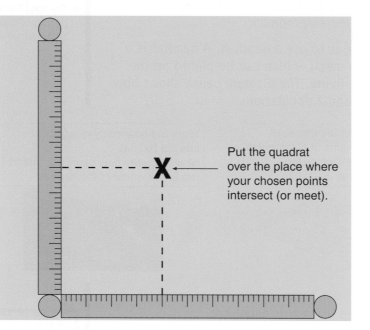

Put the quadrat over the place where your chosen points intersect (or meet).

● Count the number of chosen species (e.g. dandelion plants) within the quadrat and record the results.

Repeat this ten times, each time choosing a random location for the quadrat within the 25 m² area and recording the number of plants within it.

1 Find the average (mean) number of the plant species per quadrat. Why is it important that you take a mean rather than the first number you measured?
2 Calculate the total population of the plant species in your area. (How many times would your 0.5 m² quadrat fit into the 25 m² area?)
3 The answer you have obtained could be different from the total population measured by other groups surveying different areas have found. Suggest reasons why your findings could be different.

Go further

What about animals?

Quadrats are very easy to use with plants, like dandelions, or with animals that stay still while they are being counted (like limpets on a rocky shore). Unfortunately, animals that can move will usually run, swim or fly away while they are being counted. Luckily, there are other methods that can be used for counting animals. Here are some of the methods that can be used:

- Small animals from the soil and leaves can be collected with a form of a **Tullgren funnel**. The animals move away from the heat and dryness of the lamp. See the Investigation 'Study of a food chain...' earlier in this chapter.

- A **pitfall trap** can be used to catch small animals or insects moving across the ground. Fruit or leaves can attract herbivores or a small piece of meat could attract carnivores.

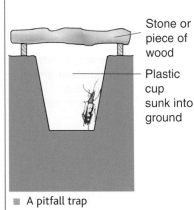

Stone or piece of wood

Plastic cup sunk into ground

■ A pitfall trap

■ A net can be used to sample flying or swimming organisms

Population curves

A population curve can be drawn by plotting the results of counting populations at different times. A population curve usually has the same shape, whichever organism is being counted. An example of a population curve is shown in the following diagram.

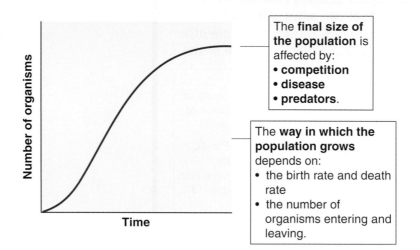

The **final size of the population** is affected by:
• **competition**
• **disease**
• **predators**.

The **way in which the population grows** depends on:
• the birth rate and death rate
• the number of organisms entering and leaving.

The shape of this curve can be understood by thinking about what a living organism needs from its environment. A habitat is an area of the environment that can provide food, shelter and breeding sites for an organism. If there is plenty of food, a number of places to shelter and no shortage of breeding sites, then the organisms can breed and new members of the same species can move into the area. The population will increase but, as this happens, the organisms become more crowded. This overcrowding will eventually mean that the population will no longer increase. There are two main reasons for this: disease and competition.

- **Disease** – As the population becomes more crowded, it becomes easier for the micro-organisms that cause disease to spread. The disease may kill some organisms and make others too unwell to breed. As a result, the population will fall. As the number of organisms falls, they spread out more, so it becomes harder for the disease to spread. The population can increase again. Usually a balance is reached, and the population size will probably become more or less constant.
- **Competition** – As the population increases, each organism has less space and less food (and less light in the case of plants) and so competition increases. Competition happens when two organisms are both trying to get the same resource from their environment. Competition for food is one of the reasons why animals try to set up a **territory**. The territory can supply them with the food, shelter and breeding sites they need. The territory will usually be small if there is plenty of food but may need to be much larger if there is very little.

8 Relationships in an ecosystem

The size of a population will also be affected by predators. There is usually a good balance between the numbers of predators and their prey (see section on 'Affecting food webs' earlier in this chapter).

Exercise 8.3: Populations

1 Twenty moose swam across a river to a large grassy island. At first, the moose population rose very rapidly, but then it levelled out. Give two reasons why the numbers stopped rising.

2 Rita wanted to discover the number of small invertebrate animals living in leaf litter (decomposing leaves) in a woodland. After obtaining her samples of leaf litter, she used this apparatus to extract the animals.

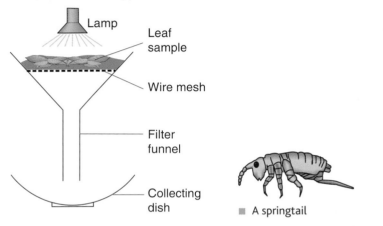

■ A springtail

(a) Suggest two reasons why the animals move into the container

Among the animals collected were a number of springtails, which feed on soil fungi. These animals have a tail that is normally folded under the body but can be released suddenly to propel the animal several centimetres forward.

(b) (i) What is the importance of fungi in the leaf litter?
   (ii) What is the advantage to the springtail of its ability to jump?

3 The graph on the right shows how the size of the population of a certain species of animal changes with time.

(a) Describe what the graph tells us.
(b) Suggest a reason for the shape of the graph.
(c) Suggest two factors that may cause the population size of an animal species to fall suddenly in its natural habitat.

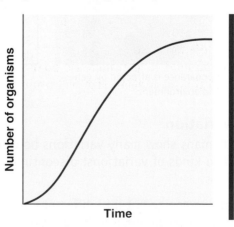

Working Scientifically

9 Variation, classification and inheritance

The variety of living organisms

Differences between living organisms are called **variations**. Even humans show variations; they come in many different shapes, sizes and colours. Just imagine how many variations humans show in such features as eye colour, skin colour, shape of earlobes and so on, and now think about how many variations there must be between humans and other species.

We can recognise different organisms more easily because of all these variations. It therefore helps in the grouping of organisms into different categories (see later in this chapter). The overall appearance of an organism is a result of the characteristics that it has **inherited** from its parents and the characteristics that result from the **effects of the environment**.

It is possible to produce an equation to summarise this:

 + 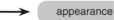 ⟶ appearance

genes + effects of the environment ⟶ appearance

The full set of information passed on from the parents

The observable characteristics of an organism

> **Remember:**
> - *All* living organisms can carry out the seven life processes (growth, nutrition, reproduction, movement, excretion, respiration and sensitivity).
> - Different organisms have different features that make them able to survive in different environments (habitats).

This girl looks like this because of the **genes** she inherited from her parents.

For example, they both have blue eyes and so does she.

She also looks like this because of the **effects of the environment**.

She has dyed her hair blonde.

She has a suntan that has darkened her skin.

■ Appearance is affected by genes and environment

Different kinds of variation

Like other organisms, humans show many variations between individuals. There are two kinds of variations: discontinuous variations and continuous variations.

- **Discontinuous variations** can be put into different groups very easily. For example, you are either blood group A, B, AB or O; there are no in-between groups. Discontinuous variations depend only on your **genes**.

- **Continuous variations** fall into many groups. These groups almost run into one another. For example, there are many groups for height or for weight. You don't just have very tall or very short people – there are many groups in between. Continuous variations depend on the environment as well as on your genes.

Blood groups A, B, AB or O

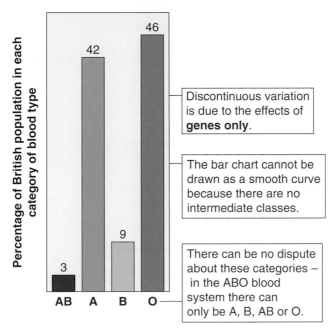

Discontinuous variation is due to the effects of **genes only**.

The bar chart cannot be drawn as a smooth curve because there are no intermediate classes.

There can be no dispute about these categories – in the ABO blood system there can only be A, B, AB or O.

■ Human blood groups are another example of discontinuous variation. You can only be in one of four distinct blood groups – AB, A, B or O – there are no in-between classes.

Nose shapes

Eye colour and shape

Hair colour and type ... face shape and freckles

■ These characteristics result from genes and are examples of discontinuous variation

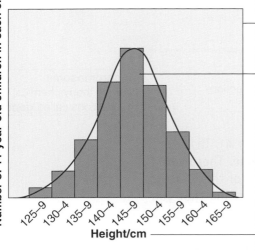

Continuous variation is due to the combined effects of **genes** and the **environment**.

The bar chart can be redrawn as a smooth curve because there are many possible intermediate classes between the two extremes. The curve becomes smoother if the classes become smaller (e.g. 1 cm rather than 5 cm).

There could be a dispute about the boundary of these classes. One observer might use, for example, 127–131, 132–6, etc. rather than the boundaries shown.

Did you know?

The importance of genes in affecting height is shown by the fact that girls are rarely, if ever, taller than their fathers. Girls do not inherit the male chromosome and this carries a gene that has a great effect on height.

■ Human height is an example of continuous variation. Other examples include quantitative characteristics such as chest circumference, body mass (weight) and hand span.

How do variations come about?

The characteristics of an organism may change **temporarily** due to some environmental effect. For example, a pale-skinned person may develop a suntan after sun exposure. These temporary variations may be of great importance to the individual organism (for example, a suntan helps to protect a human from further dangerous radiation exposure from sunlight) but they are of less importance to the species because they cannot be inherited. The characteristics that are of most interest to biologists are those that are **permanent** and *can* be inherited – eye colour and blood groups are good examples. These variations come about because of your genetic make-up, that is, what you have inherited from your parents.

Although a suntan itself cannot be inherited, the ability of the skin to produce pigments after sun exposure, can be inherited. Always think carefully about which characteristics are inherited, and which are due to the environment. Often you will find a characteristic that is both inherited and affected by the environment. For example, your height, which you inherit from your parents, is also influenced by your diet.

Genes and characteristics

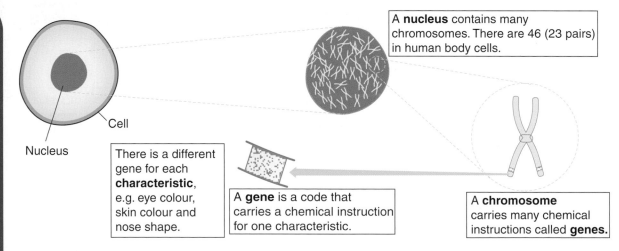

A **nucleus** contains many chromosomes. There are 46 (23 pairs) in human body cells.

Cell

Nucleus

There is a different gene for each **characteristic**, e.g. eye colour, skin colour and nose shape.

A **gene** is a code that carries a chemical instruction for one characteristic.

A **chromosome** carries many chemical instructions called **genes.**

You are the result of a fertilisation process (see Chapter 4). In fertilisation the sex cells from your two parents combine. These sex cells contain a set of genes from each parent. Because of this process, you have two sets of genes and therefore it is not surprising that you show a mixture of the characteristics of your two parents.

Fertilisation combines genes from two parents

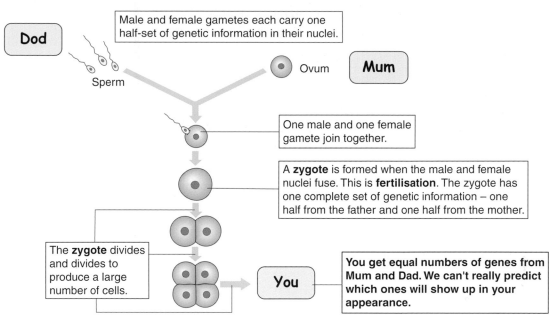

Dod

Male and female gametes each carry one half-set of genetic information in their nuclei.

Sperm

Ovum

Mum

One male and one female gamete join together.

A **zygote** is formed when the male and female nuclei fuse. This is **fertilisation**. The zygote has one complete set of genetic information – one half from the father and one half from the mother.

The **zygote** divides and divides to produce a large number of cells.

You

You get equal numbers of genes from Mum and Dad. We can't really predict which ones will show up in your appearance.

■ Fertilisation combines genes from two parents

Genes and environment also affect the characteristics of plants

Plants inherit characteristics, just as animals do. They too receive genes from the parent plants. Plants are affected much more by their environment than animals, mainly because the plants cannot move to a more suitable environment. As you know, plants are affected by four main growth factors (see Chapter 7):

- **light** – needed directly for photosynthesis and so for growth
- **temperature** – affects how quickly the chemical reactions needed for life can go on in the plant
- **water** – needed for photosynthesis and to make plant cells swell to their full size
- **minerals in the soil** – nitrate, in particular, is needed for the growth of new cells.

Investigation: Is it genes or the environment?

We can carry out experiments on sets of plants to determine whether variations are inherited or due to the environment. One of these experiments is shown here.

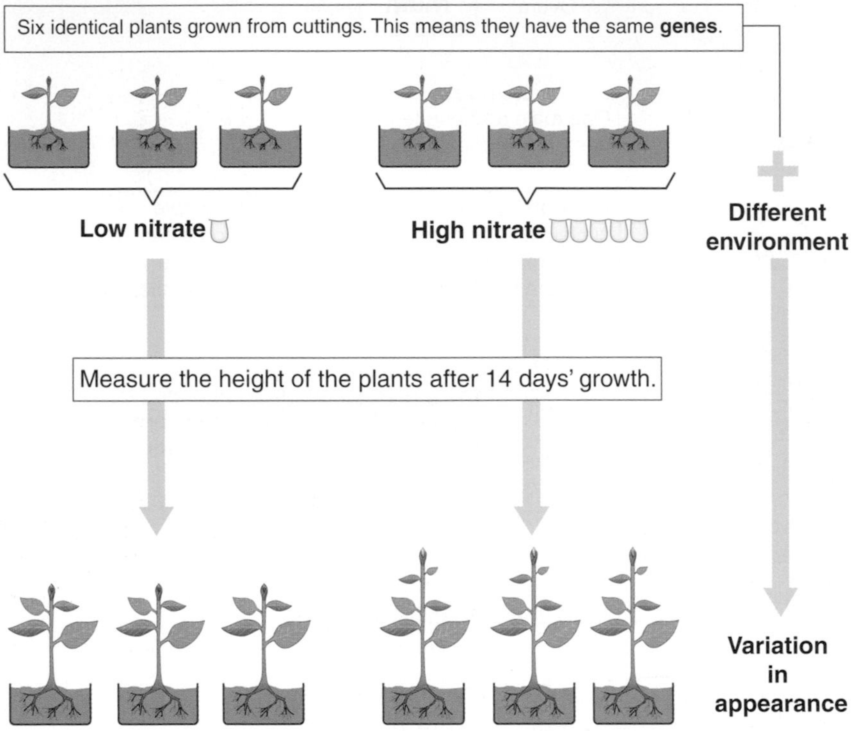

Six identical plants grown from cuttings. This means they have the same **genes**.

Low nitrate   **High nitrate**   **Different environment**

+

Measure the height of the plants after 14 days' growth.

Variation in appearance

Make certain that the only environmental factor that is altered is the **amount of nitrate**.

1 What other environmental factors must be kept constant to make this a fair test?
2 What conclusion would you draw from these results?

It is not so easy to carry out experiments like this on animals but sometimes they are important. For example, a food company might want to test whether a new food helps growth or not. Scientists can now produce batches of identical animals called **clones**. The animals can then be fed with different amounts of the new food and their growth measured. Because these animals have identical genes, any difference in growth must be due to the different amounts of food.

Do you think it is acceptable to use animals in this way? Discuss this with a partner.

Differences exist between species

Discontinuous variations may be so great that they result in different species. For example, the great apes (chimpanzees, gorillas and orang-utans) share a common ancestor with humans but there are enough differences between them to mean that they are separate species. Scientists have always had some problems with deciding *exactly* what is meant by the term species.

- Traditionally, two organisms were not from the same species if they could not interbreed and produce fertile offspring.
- Modern biology suggests that organisms are from different species if they have enough differences in the shape and number of their **chromosomes** (humans have 46 chromosomes, chimpanzees have 48, for example) and in the genes they carry on these chromosomes.

Charles Darwin and Alfred Russel Wallace

Charles Darwin (1809–82) was an English naturalist who studied variation in plants and animals during a five-year voyage around the world on a ship called HMS *Beagle*. His voyage began in 1831 and he studied finches, iguanas and mockingbirds, among other species, on the Galapagos Islands. Darwin made very careful observations of many **adaptations** (characteristics suited to environment) of species, and began to suggest how these adaptations could have arisen. Alfred Russel Wallace (1823–1913) was a British professional animal collector working in Malaysia. He also made many observations on adaptation, and wrote to Darwin to describe some of his ideas. Darwin realised that Wallace had reached the same conclusions as he had. This spurred Darwin on to publish his ideas, and he explained his ideas on adaptation and evolution (the gradual changing of a species over a long time) in a book called *On the Origin of Species*, published in 1859.

The main features in his theory are that:

- individuals compete for limited resources
- individuals in a population show natural variation
- individuals with characteristics best suited to their environment (adaptations) are more likely to survive to reproduce. Darwin called this natural selection.
- 'successful' characteristics are inherited (although Darwin knew nothing at all about genes and how they control characteristics).

Darwin's ideas caused a lot of controversy, and this continues today. They can be seen as conflicting with religious views about the creation of the world and the creatures in it.

Darwin's theory is now supported by our understanding of genes and fossil evidence (see later in this chapter).

■ These four animals are all primates; they each have thumbs and forward-facing eyes, for example. They have between 96% and 98% of the same DNA (think how many similarities there are: number of limbs, kidneys that concentrate urine and colour vision, for example) but they are certainly different species!

Natural selection

As Darwin's theory explains, some individuals within a species are better suited to their environment than others. These individuals will be more likely to survive and breed than some of their competitors. Because of this, the characteristics they possess will become more common in the species over many generations. This process is called **natural selection**.

One well-known example of natural selection concerns a type of moth called a peppered moth (*Biston betularia*). These moths are either pale or dark. Before the industrial revolution in Britain in the late-eighteenth century, the pale moths were more common. Their natural habitat was on the pale trunks of trees. The pale moths were better camouflaged and not eaten as often by small birds as the dark moths. Numbers of the dark moths stayed low as they were likely to be eaten before they could reproduce.

The industrial revolution caused pollution, which blackened tree trunks. The darker moths were now better camouflaged than the pale moths. The camouflaged dark moths had a better chance of survival than the pale moths and therefore had a better chance of reproducing and passing on their 'dark' genes (and characteristics) to the next generation. Over several generations the proportion of dark moths increased and the proportion of the pale moths decreased.

Go further

Natural selection can lead to new species when populations become isolated or separated. One example of this occurs in antelopes. A common ancestor of different antelopes might have shown continuous variation in height and coat colour. Different selection pressures, such as the availability of food or the presence of predators, might favour different combinations of characteristics in different populations of antelopes. If the two populations are separated, by a mountain range or river for example, after a period of time they might have so many different adaptations that they can no longer interbreed; they are now different species.

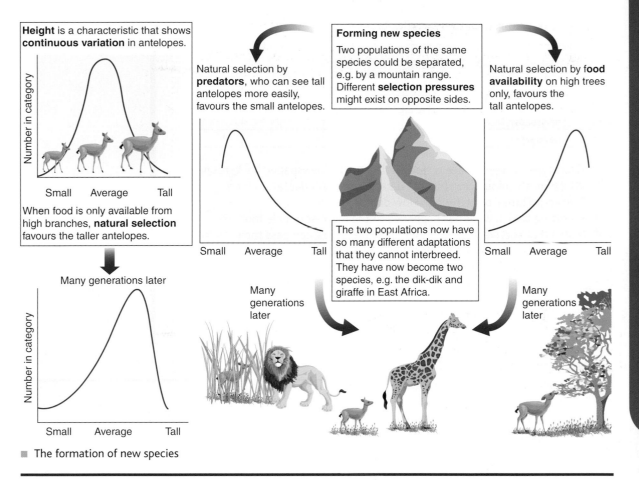

Height is a characteristic that shows continuous variation in antelopes.

When food is only available from high branches, natural selection favours the taller antelopes.

Many generations later

Natural selection by predators, who can see tall antelopes more easily, favours the small antelopes.

Forming new species

Two populations of the same species could be separated, e.g. by a mountain range. Different selection pressures might exist on opposite sides.

Natural selection by food availability on high trees only, favours the tall antelopes.

The two populations now have so many different adaptations that they cannot interbreed. They have now become two species, e.g. the dik-dik and giraffe in East Africa.

Many generations later

Many generations later

■ The formation of new species

Investigation: Modelling natural selection

In this investigation you will simulate how predators locate prey and analyse how camouflage (colour and patterns) affect an organism's ability to survive in certain environments.

Work in pairs. Place a sheet of white paper on the table – the paper represents a tree trunk. Your teacher will give you 30 small white paper circles and 30 small newspaper circles (made using a hole punch) – these represent pale and dark moths. One of you should scatter the small circles over the piece of paper while the other (the 'predator') looks away.

The 'predator' should now use forceps to pick up as many of the circles as he/she can in 15 seconds. This simulates a predator capturing and eating the prey species.

Repeat this simulation once more.

Do this simulation twice more – this time with the circles on a newspaper background.

Make a copy of this table and record your results:

Trial	Background	Starting population		Number 'eaten'	
		Newspaper	White	Newspaper	White
1	white	30	30		
2	white	30	30		
3	newspaper	30	30		
4	newspaper	30	30		

1 What type of tree surface is represented by the 'newspaper' background?
2 Which moth colouration (pale or dark) is the best adaptation for a 'smoke-polluted' background? How do you know?
3 Following trial 1, what has happened to the number of pale moths?
4 Moths that survive, i.e. are not eaten by predators, can pass their colouration characteristic when they reproduce. How does the simulation model natural selection?

Extension question

5 Hospital managers are very worried about hospital infections. Explain how natural selection might lead to antibiotic-resistant strains of bacteria.

Go further

Changes in the environment may cause extinction of species

The environment can only supply limited resources, such as food or places to shelter. The organisms in the environment compete for these limited resources, and some are less successful than others. Over a long period a species may become well adapted to its environment because it is successful at competing for resources, but then may suffer if the environment changes!

Some important examples are shown in the pictures on the right. All of these species have suffered as a result of changes in their environment.

■ Neanderthal man (*Homo neanderthalis*) lived in Europe around 50 000 years ago, but could not compete with modern man (*Homo sapiens*) who hunted more efficiently and formed better social groups.

■ The polar bear is suffering as a result of a warming climate that has reduced the amount of pack ice in the Arctic, the polar bear's natural habitat.

■ The dodo could not survive after its home in Mauritius was overtaken by settlers who cut down the dodo's forest habitat and introduced cats and rats, which ate the bird's eggs.

When a species has no living members left, it is said to be extinct – like Neanderthal man and the dodo. The polar bear is classified as a 'threatened' species due to its reduced numbers.

◯ Evolution and inheritance

As we have seen, living species change through time (and may eventually produce new species). This changing through time is called **evolution**. Evolution occurs over very, very long periods of time – for example, evidence from fossils suggests that it took many millions of years for the modern-day form of the horse to evolve.

Fossils are formed when the bodies of dead animals do not decompose but are instead turned into rock. The best fossils are found in sedimentary rock, which were formed from sediments such as sand or mud at the bottom of ancient seas. The oldest sedimentary rocks, and therefore the oldest fossils, are found in the deepest layers of rock.

1 Organisms die – bodies sink to the bottom of the sea and become covered in sediment.

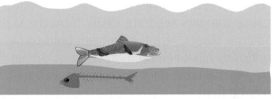

2 Sediment hardens and the remains turn to stone. New layers, containing newer remains, form over the old.

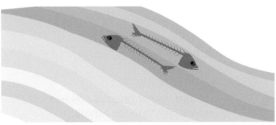

3 Rock layers (strata) fold and are raised up out of the sea. They are now exposed to wind and rain.

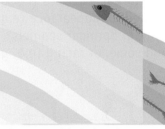

4 Erosion, and faults in rocks, expose the different strata and the fossils they contain.

Mary Anning

The greatest fossil hunter ever known was a woman from Lyme Regis, called Mary Anning (1799–1847). Mary's father, Richard, collected fossils. They were cleaned, polished, and sold to summer tourists. After her father's death, Mary's fossil discoveries were some of the most significant geological finds of all time. They provided evidence that was very important in the development of new ideas about the history of the Earth and prompted the scientific community into looking at different explanations for the changes in the natural world that we now call evolution.

■ Ichthyosaurus fossil

In 1811 or 1812, Anning was responsible for the finding of a well-preserved, nearly complete skeleton of what came to be called an Ichthyosaurus ('fish-lizard'). This discovery was important to science as well as to Anning's livelihood.

In 1823, Anning made another important discovery, perhaps her greatest. She found the first complete Plesiosaurus ('near lizard'). This was a reptile that was nine feet long and lived in the sea. It had a long neck, short tail, small head, and four flippers that were pointed and shaped like paddles. They were very rare, and Anning's discovery led to the identification of a new genus.

■ Plesiosaurus

Selective breeding

Variation occurs naturally in all living organisms. This means that they have different characteristics. It is possible to deliberately select and mix characteristics to produce varieties of animals and plants that are useful to humans.

Ever since early humans began to domesticate animals and plants, they have been trying to improve them. This improvement is brought about by choosing or selecting individual organisms with the most useful characteristics, and allow these individuals to reproduce (breed). This process is called **selective breeding**, here are some examples:

■ Pedigree dogs come in lots of different varieties (breeds)

- Wheat has been bred so that all the stems are the same height. This makes harvesting easier and makes collection of the grain easier because the ears separate easily from the stalk. Like many other food crop plants, it has also been bred to be disease resistant.
- Cauliflower has been bred for its large edible flower (see next page).
- Jersey cattle have been bred to produce milk with a very high cream content.
- Aberdeen Angus cattle have been bred to produce higher quality beef.
- All domestic dogs are the same *species* (*Canis lupus familiaris*) but some have been bred for appearance (e.g. Pekinese), some as hunting companions (e.g. Springer spaniels), some as guard dogs (e.g. Rottweilers) and some for racing (e.g. greyhounds, see below).

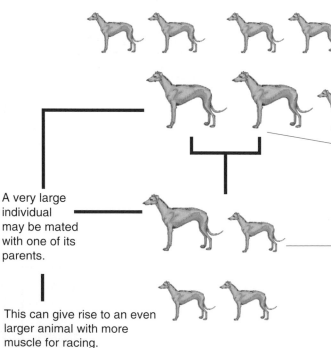

In this litter of greyhounds two are larger than the others. Large greyhounds carry more muscle, which is valuable to a racing animal.

These two dogs with the desirable characteristic are allowed to breed and produce a litter.

A very large individual may be mated with one of its parents.

If the size characteristic is inherited, the next generation may contain individuals that are even bigger.

This can give rise to an even larger animal with more muscle for racing.

■ Selective breeding of animals

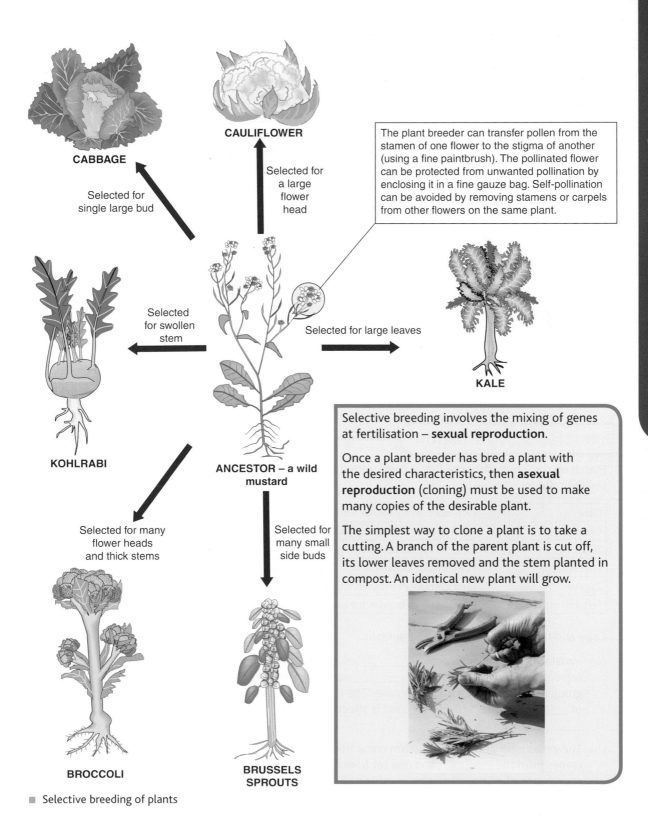

CABBAGE

Selected for
single large bud

CAULIFLOWER

Selected for
a large
flower
head

The plant breeder can transfer pollen from the
stamen of one flower to the stigma of another
(using a fine paintbrush). The pollinated flower
can be protected from unwanted pollination by
enclosing it in a fine gauze bag. Self-pollination
can be avoided by removing stamens or carpels
from other flowers on the same plant.

Selected
for swollen
stem

Selected for large leaves

KALE

KOHLRABI

**ANCESTOR – a wild
mustard**

Selected for many
flower heads
and thick stems

Selected for
many small
side buds

Selective breeding involves the mixing of genes
at fertilisation – **sexual reproduction**.

Once a plant breeder has bred a plant with
the desired characteristics, then **asexual
reproduction** (cloning) must be used to make
many copies of the desirable plant.

The simplest way to clone a plant is to take a
cutting. A branch of the parent plant is cut off,
its lower leaves removed and the stem planted in
compost. An identical new plant will grow.

BROCCOLI

**BRUSSELS
SPROUTS**

■ Selective breeding of plants

Of course, what humans consider a valuable characteristic might not actually be valuable in a natural situation. A pet animal such as a Chihuahua dog would probably not survive in the wild because its hunting instincts have been bred out to make it a more desirable pet.

Characteristics that can be selectively bred are controlled by genes (see earlier in this chapter). However, it is important that humans preserve unpopular genes, i.e. genes that do not currently offer any advantage to us. It may be that a cow with a very limited milk yield in fact carries a gene that makes it resistant to a disease that is not yet a problem in domestic herds. Such a gene would be extremely valuable if such a disease ever did threaten herds of cows. For this reason, many less useful varieties of animals and plants are kept in small numbers in **rare breed centres** across the country and overseas. Plant genes may be conserved in their seeds, which make them easy to store. **Seed banks** are stores of large numbers of different plant varieties. Some animal genes may be stored as frozen eggs, sperm and embryos.

Do you think it is *always* acceptable for humans to use selective breeding? When do you think it might be unacceptable?

Exercise 9.1: Variation

1 Match up the words from the first column with the definitions from the second column.

Gene	A process that joins sex cells together
Chromosome	All factors affecting an organism
Variation	The first cell that contains genes from two parents
Environment	Determines a characteristic of an organism
Zygote	The differences between organisms
Fertilisation	A thin strand, found in the nucleus, that carries a set of genes

2 Copy and complete the following paragraphs.

(a) Variation occurs in two forms. _____ variation shows clear cut separation between groups, and _____ variation, which comprises groups that almost run into each other. The first of these is the result of _____ alone, while the second is affected by both _____ and _____ factors.

(b) The genes inherited by an organism come from its _____. One set comes from the _____ and one set from the _____. The overall appearance of an organism can be explained in a simple equation: _____ plus _____ equals _____.

3 Which of the following is an example of discontinuous variation?

body mass, chest circumference, blood group, hairstyle, height.

(a) Explain why you chose this alternative.

(b) Explain why you rejected the others.

Extension question

4 Two students in the first year of secondary school were carrying out a mathematical investigation. They decided to measure the heights of all the other students in their class. Here are their results:

Height category/cm	Number in category
121–125	2
126–130	4
131–135	9
136–140	6
141–145	4
146–150	1

(a) Plot these results as a bar chart.

(b) Explain how these differences in height could have come about.

(c) Suggest one characteristic that the students could have studied that would have given only two different groups.

◯ Preliminary knowledge: Putting living things into groups

Living organisms show variation, which means there are physical differences between them. Scientists can use these differences to produce **keys**.

A key is a set of questions that we can ask for ourselves. The questions should be based on biological features and features that are easy to see. Each question should have two possible answers. The answer to one question leads on to another question. This goes on until the name of the organism is found.

One kind of key is called a **branching key** or **spider key**, and an example is shown on the next page. Try to use this branching key to classify all of the organisms shown at the top.

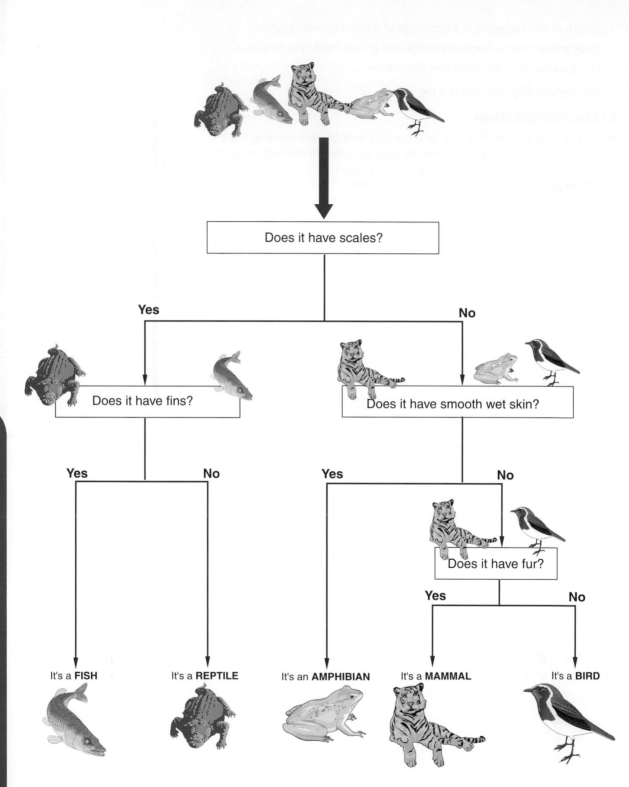

Branching keys can take up a lot of space. The way to get around this problem is to use a numbered key. In a numbered key, each question is given a number. The answer to the question may send you to another number. Try using this numbered key to classify these invertebrates:

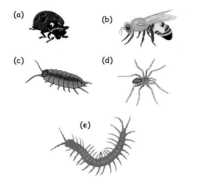

KEY:

1.	Does it have 6 legs?	YES	Go to question 2.
		NO	Go to question 3.
2.	Does it have hard cases for its wings?	YES	It's a ladybird.
		NO	It's a bee.
3.	Does it have 8 legs?	YES	It's a spider.
		NO	Go to question 4.
4.	Does it have more than 20 legs?	YES	It's a centipede.
		NO	It's a woodlouse.

Classification

We know that a key is a very useful way to identify living things. A key works by asking a set of questions about the features an organism has. The answers we give to the questions begin to split up a large group of living things into individual organisms.

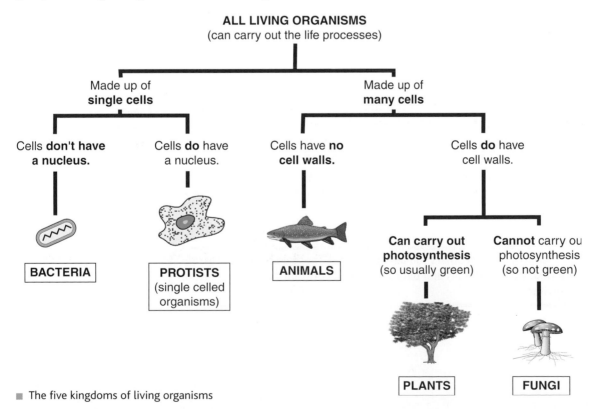

■ The five kingdoms of living organisms

Scientists can use the answers to these questions to put all known living organisms into groups, by grouping together all the organisms with similar features. This system of grouping together living organisms is called **classification**.

All living organisms can be put into very large groups called **kingdoms**. There are five kingdoms and every living organism can be placed into one or other of them.

The animal kingdom

All the animals in the world can be put into one of two groups: **vertebrates** or **invertebrates**. We can put animals into the correct group by answering just one question:

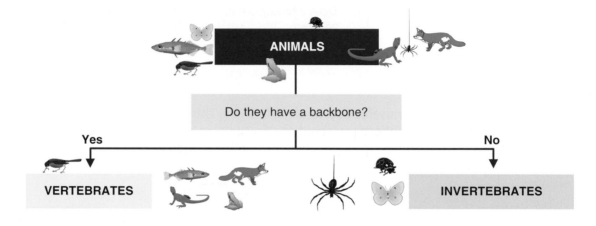

Vertebrates

There are many times more invertebrates than vertebrates, but most of us recognise vertebrates more easily. There are five groups of vertebrates; mammals, birds, amphibians, fish and reptiles. We can generally recognise the five groups by looking at their skin (see the branching key on the next page), although there are other important differences between the groups. These are summarised in the table on the next page.

> Vertebrates don't just have a backbone; they have a complete bony skeleton.

> Fur (on mammals) and feathers (on birds) are vital. These coverings act as insulation, so that mammals and birds can keep a constant body temperature in the environment.

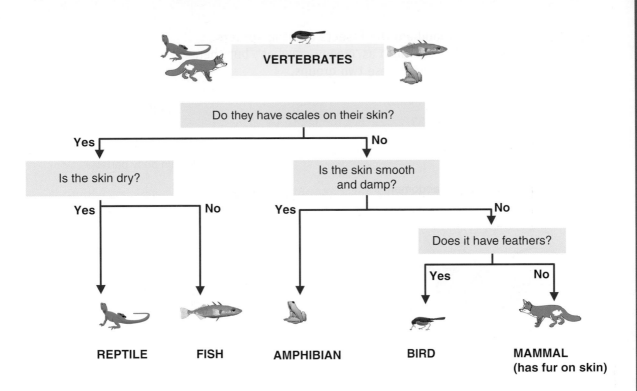

■ Other important differences of vertebrates

	REPTILE	FISH	AMPHIBIAN	BIRD	MAMMAL
Constant body temperature	No	No	No	Yes	Yes
Does it lay eggs?	Yes – with soft shells	Yes – in water	Yes – in water	Yes – with hard shells	No
Does it feed its young on milk?	No	No	No	No	Yes

Humans are vertebrates, and belong to the class called the **mammals**.

Invertebrates

As you have seen, the invertebrates are animals without backbones. It is not always easy to tell that they haven't got backbones because some of them have very hard covers on their bodies. This hard body is good for protection against predators, but can make movement difficult. To make movement easier, one group of invertebrates, called the **arthropods**, consists of animals that have many joints in their limbs (the word arthropod actually means 'jointed foot').

Two different kinds of arthropod are the **insects** and the **spiders**.
Some people would classify them both as 'creepy-crawlies', but there
are important differences between these two groups.

INSECT	**SPIDER**

Three main body parts:

head   thorax   abdomen

1 pair of
antennae

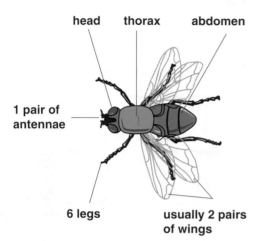

6 legs   usually 2 pairs
              of wings

Two main body parts:

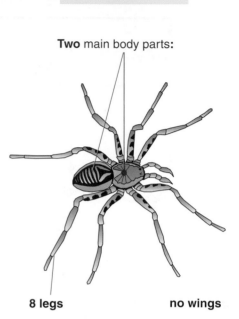

8 legs   no wings

Did you know?

No matter how hard we've tried, humans have
never managed to wipe out an insect pest species.
(We have killed off some non-harmful species by
accident though.)

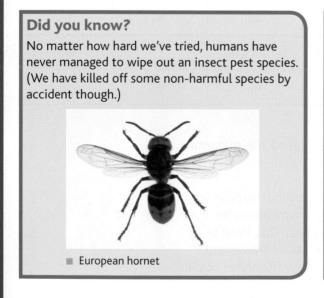

■ European hornet

Did you know?

Every spider is a meat-eater – there are no
herbivores.

■ Mexican red-leg tarantula

The plant kingdom

All plants have one thing in common: they have a pigment that can absorb light energy, so that they can make their own food by photosynthesis. We can divide up all the plants into two main groups, by asking just one question.

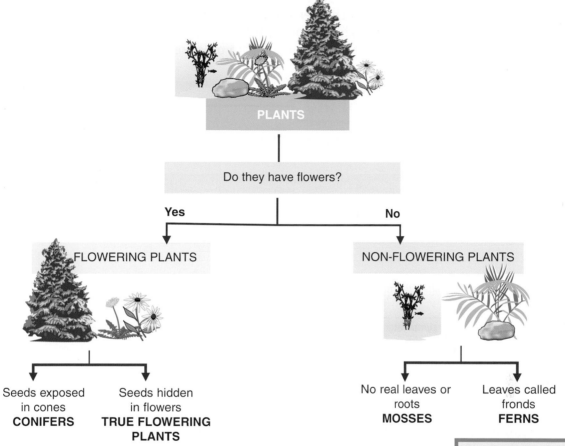

Scientists used to believe that fungi were plants. They thought this because they knew fungi definitely were not animals. In fact, even though mushrooms and toadstools look more like plants than animals, *fungi cannot carry out photosynthesis and so cannot be called plants.*

> Non-flowering plants never make seeds — instead they reproduce with tiny structures called **spores**.

Did you know?

Fungi have no chlorophyll, so must feed by digesting other foods.

They use enzymes (just like humans do) to decompose animals and plants, or their remains.

Fungi are therefore not plants, nor are they animals. Can you explain this to your parents?

What is a species?

There are many other questions that can be asked to split these large groups (kingdoms) into smaller and smaller groups. The smallest of all groups is called the **species**. Members of the same species are so much alike that males and females can mate and produce offspring just like themselves (see earlier in this chapter – 'How do variations come about?' – for information about chromosomes, DNA and species).

Humans are one species, oak trees are another and barn owls are another and so on.

Exercise 9.2: The variety of life

1 Copy this table. Use information from this section to fill in the gaps. Put a '+' if a feature is present and a '−' if it is absent.

Feature	Fish	Amphibian	Reptile	Bird	Mammal
Backbone					
Scales					
Feathers					
Hairy skin					

2 Match up the description from the first column with the group from the second column.

Has wings, a constant body temperature and lays eggs with hard shells	Insect
Has no backbone, two body parts and eight jointed legs	Fungus
Has a body made of a single cell with a clear nucleus and cytoplasm	Fish
Has no backbone, three body parts and six jointed legs	Mammal
Has cells with a definite cell wall but does not feed by photosynthesis	Flowering plant
Has hair, provides milk for its young and has a constant body temperature	Protist
Has a backbone, gills, fins and scales	Bird
Has flowers for reproduction and green leaves	Spider

Extension question

3 The system for giving all living things a name in Latin was suggested by a scientist called Carl Linnaeus in the eighteenth century.

(a) Use the internet or your library to copy and complete this table.

Latin name	Common name
Fraxinus excelsior	
	English oak
Pan troglodytes	
Loxodonta africana	
	Foxglove
	Common frog

(b) What is the advantage of a common system of names?

(c) Try to find the name for the lion in French, German and Swahili.

Carl Linnaeus

Carl Linnaeus is famous for his work in taxonomy, the science of identifying, naming and classifying organisms. He was born in 1707, the eldest of five children, in Sweden. His father was a keen gardener and would often take his young son Carl into the garden with him and teach him about botany (the study of plants). By the age of five, Carl had his own garden, which gave him a great thirst for learning about plants and how they work.

His father taught Carl that every plant had a name. Plant names (which were in Latin, and still are to this day) were very long and descriptive, and difficult to remember, but Carl dedicated himself to learning as many as he could.

In 1728, after spending a year studying medicine at the University of Lund, Carl Linnaeus transferred to Uppsala University, where he studied the use of plants, minerals and animals in medicine.

From 1732 to 1735, Linnaeus travelled throughout Sweden in order to record and collect information on the country's natural resources. Linnaeus used his new binomial system of naming to describe the plants and animals he found on his travels.

Linnaeus was both popular and influential as a professor and scientist. It was due to his influence that the Royal Navy sent naturalists on all their voyages, including Charles Darwin. Not only is Linnaeus considered the 'Father of Taxonomy', he was also a pioneer in the study of ecology. He was one of the first to describe relationships between living things and their environments.

Glossary

Adaptation   the process of gradual change by which a species becomes better suited to its environment.

Addiction   the body's dependence on a drug to such an extent that it can no longer function properly or carry on a normal life without it.

Adequate diet   nutrients to supply sufficient energy to drive all of the life processes.

Adolescence   the period of human development at around aged 10 to 20, where physical and emotional changes occur to ready the person for reproduction.

Aerobic   in the presence of oxygen.

Amniotic fluid   liquid inside the amniotic sac that surrounds the developing fetus.

Amniotic sac   the membranous bag of amniotic fluid inside the womb where the fetus develops and grows.

Antibodies   proteins made by some white blood cells that can defend the body against micro-organisms.

Asthma   a condition in which the airways constrict and make breathing difficult.

Balanced diet   all the nutrients in the correct proportions.

Biodiversity   the range of different living organisms.

Biomass   material made by the process of photosynthesis and built into the body of a plant.

Breathing   the movements that bring air in and out of the lungs.

Cancer   a disease in which cells begin to divide out of control and harm normal body tissues.

Carbon cycle   a set of chemical reactions that follow what happens to carbon dioxide and sugars in the environment; it links photosynthesis and respiration.

Cell   a building block of a living organism.

Chlorophyll   the green pigment in plant cells that can absorb light energy for photosynthesis.

Chloroplast   the structure in the plant cell where photosynthesis takes place.

Chromosome   a thread inside the nucleus of a cell; it is made of many genes.

Classification   a way of placing living organisms into groups with similar characteristics.

Competition   two or more organisms seeking the same resource from the environment.

Conception   the beginning of the development of a new individual.

Conservation   managing the environment for the benefit of wildlife.

Consumer   an organism that obtains its food energy by eating another organism.

Continuous variation   differences that can easily overlap, for example, body mass.

Copulation   sexual intercourse; the time when the sperm from the male are delivered to the female's reproductive system.

Decomposer   an organism that can break down molecules from the bodies of other 'dead' organisms.

Deficiency disease   a disease caused by the lack of a particular nutrient in the diet.

Deforestation   cutting down large areas of trees.

Development   (of cells) the changes of cells that mean some of them take on different functions.

Diaphragm   muscle that contracts to help the chest get bigger during breathing in.

Diet   all the nutrients supplied to the body.

Diffusion   the spreading or mixing of a substance by natural movement of its particles.

Discontinuous variation   differences that fall into very clear classes, for example, male and female.

DNA   the molecule that makes up genes and chromosomes and so controls the characteristics of an organism.

Drug   any chemical that alters the activities of the body.

Embryo   a stage of development when the ball of cells begins to rearrange itself so that some organs can be seen.

Enzyme   a biological molecule that can speed up a reaction.

Evolution   the theory that new species form from previous ones over many generations due to natural selection.

Extinction   the complete loss of a species, often as a result of competition for resources with better adapted species.

Fertilisation   the joining together of sperm and egg.

Fertiliser   a group of minerals added to soil to help plant growth.

Fitness   the ability to deliver oxygen to working muscles efficiently.

Food chain   the flow of food energy between living organisms.

Food web   a set of different food chains that overlap and link up with one another.

Fossil   the remains or impression of an organism preserved in rock.

Gametes   special sex cells, the sperm and the egg.

Genes   sections of the chromosomes that control the characteristics of living organisms.

Germination   the process by which a plant grows from a seed.

Gestation period   the length of time between fertilisation and birth.

Greenhouse   an environment where the ideal conditions for photosynthesis can be created.

Growth   getting bigger by the production of more cells.

Habitat   a part of the environment that can provide food, shelter and a breeding site.

Immunity   when the body has antibodies ready to fight off an infection by a micro-organism.

Infectious   a disease that can be passed on to another person.

Intercostal muscles   muscles between the ribs that contract to lift up the ribcage during breathing.

Invertebrate   an animal without a backbone.

Iodine   a chemical that reacts with starch to give a blue-black colour.

Joule   the unit of energy (1 kilojoule equals 1000 Joules).

Kingdom   a very large classification group, for example, the animal kingdom.

Limewater   solution that turns cloudy (sometimes described as milky/chalky) when carbon dioxide is bubbled through it.

Lymphocyte   a white blood cell that produces antibodies.

Malnutrition   the result of not receiving the correct balance of foods.

Medicine   a drug used to treat or prevent an illness.

Menstruation   the release of the bloody lining of the uterus if no fertilisation has taken place.

Micro-organism   an organism that can only be seen under a microscope.

Microscope   an instrument that can be used to magnify very small objects, such as cells.

Multicellular   organism made up of many cells.

Natural selection   the process in which organisms that are better adapted to their environment have a better chance of surviving and reproducing.

Nicotine   the substance in tobacco that causes addiction – it also speeds up the heart rate.

Nitrate   a common mineral in fertilisers – it is needed by plants for the production of proteins.

Non-infectious   a disease that cannot be passed from one person to another.

Obesity   where the body is so overweight that disease is more likely to occur.

Organ   several tissues working together.

Organ system   several organs that are connected to one another, so that one job can be carried out very efficiently.

Organism   an individual living thing.

Ovulation   the maturation and release of an ovum (egg cell) from the ovary.

Paranoia   a mental condition characterised by untrue feelings of ill treatment.

Phagocyte   a type of white blood cell that can engulf and digest micro-organisms.

Photosynthesis   the process by which green plants use sunlight to make nutrients from carbon dioxide and water.

Placenta   a structure linking the umbilical cord to the wall of the uterus.

Pollination   the transfer of pollen from the anther (male part) to the stigma (female part) of the plant, enabling fertilisation and reproduction.

Pollution   the introduction into the environment of a substance that is harmful to the environment or to organisms.

Population   all the members of the same species living in one area.

Predator   an animal that chases and catches other animals (prey) for food.

Prey   an animal that is caught and killed for food by another animal (predator).

Producer   an organism that can trap light energy to supply food energy to a food chain.

Puberty   the stage of adolescence in human development at which the person develops the physical characteristics to be able to reproduce.

Quadrat   a wooden or metal square that can be used in the counting of populations.

Respiration   the release of energy from food molecules.

Selective breeding   the process by which humans breed animals and plants for particular characteristics.

Sex hormones   chemicals that control the physical and mental changes at adolescence.

Sexual intercourse   copulation; the time when the sperm from the male are delivered to the female's reproductive system.

Sexual reproduction   the production of new individuals with a combination of features from two parents.

Signs   what a doctor looks for in a patient with a disease.

Specialisation   how cells change their structure, so that they can carry out particular functions.

Species   a very small classification group; the organisms in it are so similar to each other that they can breed with one another.

Starch   a large carbohydrate molecule and the food store in many plant tissues.

Starvation   a severe lack of the nutrients needed to maintain life.

Sustainable development   only taking enough from the environment to make sure that there will be some left for future generations.

Symptoms   what a patient feels like when he has a disease.

Tissue   a collection of cells that look the same and carry out the same function.

Umbilical cord   the structure that links the developing fetus to the placenta.

Unicellular   organism made up of only one cell.

Variable   something (a factor) that changes during the course of an experiment.

Vertebrate   an structure with a backbone.

Zygote   the structure formed when a sperm and an egg combine.

Index